Pastoral Theology
in an
Intercultural World

WITHDRAWN

Pastoral Theology in an Intercultural World

Emmanuel Y. Lartey

✦ EPWORTH

British Library Cataloguing in Publication data

A catalogue record for this book is available
from the British Library

0 7162 0583 1/
978 0 7162 0583 8

First published in 2006
by Epworth
4 John Wesley Road
Werrington
Peterborough PE4 6ZP

Printed and bound in Great Britain by
William Clowes Ltd, Beccles, Suffolk

Contents

Acknowledgements

The drafting and crafting of this book have taken place over a period of almost nine years. I was first approached by the Revd Gerald Burt, then Editorial Secretary of Epworth Press, in February 1997 to consider writing a book on Pastoral Theology to be published in Epworth's *Groundwork* series. Many thanks are due to Revd Burt, who continued steadfastly to encourage me, after my affirmative response, over several years until his retirement from that position in 2003. Natalie Watson became commissioning editor at that time, and continued the task of pursuing and encouraging an over-extended author to complete the text to which I had committed myself. Dr Watson is also to be credited for recognizing that the text that had emerged might do better as a stand-alone title. I am indebted to her for negotiating its release from the series, and overseeing the final stages of its preparation.

My thanks are due posthumously to the Revd Dr J. Michael Wilson, whose poetry may be found in Chapter 4, for his dedicated and exemplary love, care and mentoring. His widow, Jean Wilson, deserves my thanks also for her unfailing support from their home in Birmingham over all these years.

I wish to thank faculty colleagues and students of the Department of Theology at the University of Birmingham, especially those present from 1989, when I returned there to be Lecturer in Pastoral Studies, and through the years 1997–2001 during my tenure there, for providing me with a collegial environment of support and critique, where it was possible to develop some of the crucial ideas within this book. Graduate students in Pastoral Studies of several nationalities enriched my thinking through our seminars and discussions during those years. In that regard it was my privilege and joy to be granted a sabbatical by the university in the Fall Semester of 2000 primarily to work on this book. I am forever grateful to my friend and kindred spirit Dr Jim Poling of Garrett-Evangelical Theological Seminary in Evanston, Illinois, for arranging for me to spend that sabbatical at Garrett as Scholar-in-Residence. The extremely cold weather, together with the warmth and cordiality of faculty colleagues in Chicago, made my stay there both academically productive and enjoyable.

I thank Dr Anthony Reddie of Queens Theological Foundation, Birmingham, for constant encouragement, and also the participants at the monthly seminars of the Black Theology Study Group for many invigorating discussions.

During October 2001–December 2004, while serving on the Faculty at Columbia Theological Seminary, I was the beneficiary of research funds from the Griffith Theological Research Foundation, Inc., which enabled me to engage the research assistance of Beth Toler, currently a doctoral student in Pastoral Counselling at Emory University. I am grateful to the foundation for funding and Beth for her valuable research work. I am grateful to colleagues at Columbia Seminary and Pastoral Counselling doctoral students in the Atlanta Theological Association's ThD programme for allowing me the opportunity to explore some of these ideas with you all.

I would like to salute my faculty colleagues, staff and students at Candler School of Theology and the Graduate Division of Religion at Emory University, sites of my teaching, research and service since January 2005, for the stimulating environment they have provided for the completion and final tasks towards the publication of this book.

To Hannah Ward and Kenneth Burnley for proof reading, Mary Matthews, Editorial Manager at SCM-Canterbury Press, and the folk at Pilgrim Press, go my sincere thanks.

ACKNOWLEDGEMENTS

Thanks go to my spouse and dear friend, Griselda, for her undying support and to our family of young men – Theo, Henry, Junior and Wesley – for bearing with the strange antics of an academic author's faltering steps as father.

Finally, I give honour to God and my ancestors, especially my maternal grandfather Christian A. Doku and grandmother Augusta B. Doku, and to my mother Doris Christiana Lartey (1917–2000) to whom this book is dedicated.

Emmanuel Y. Lartey
Atlanta, Georgia
2006

Introduction

Flora is 52 and lives in England. She is of West African origin though she has lived in the UK for most of her life. She is contemplating moving back permanently to live 'at home' in West Africa, though she wonders whether she will 'fit' any longer. She makes it a point to visit her home country at least every other year with a view to keeping in touch with cultural and social developments. Flora was a highly successful professional social worker and social work educator, enjoyed her work and is deeply committed to the wellbeing of those around her. She is also active in her local church, while also supportive of her church in West Africa, sending financial contributions there for the annual church harvest thanksgiving each year. 'Spirituality is basic to our humanity' is a statement she often makes with conviction to her pastoral counsellor. Flora's father was an ordained minister in the Methodist Church. He died while she was a high school student. Her mother died three years ago. Flora has three younger sisters and had two brothers. The one brother who was older than her died tragically of an 'undiagnosed' condition just a year ago. Flora had a difficult relationship with her mother but got on fabulously with her maternal grandfather – an educationist and widely respected churchman.

Flora is divorced after 12 years of marriage to an Englishman who turned out to be 'alcoholic, physically abusive and unfaithful'. She suffered several miscarriages in the early years of her marriage and does not have a child of her own. Flora's medical doctor has recently diagnosed her as having a 'chronic, inflammatory autoimmune disorder that may affect many organs including the skin, joints and internal organs, which affects Africans, Asians and African Americans more often than other races'. She is suffering depression, constant bodily pain and loss of energy. Six months ago she lost her job following vindictive accusations that later proved to be false.

Flora has set up sessions with the minister of her local Methodist church in London because she feels 'a loss of personal and spiritual direction in life'. She also suffers feelings of abandonment. She has joined a yoga and meditation class to which she was introduced by an Asian former co-worker. The Asian woman leader of this class is a licensed psychotherapist who helps people devise their own healing rituals. Flora finds the eastern religious meditative practice very soothing. Flora also 'goes for prayers' with a West African woman who has a prayer ministry in south London. She describes these prayers and the other ritual activities that go with them as 'dynamic and spiritual, in tune with my African roots'.

Recently Flora has been thinking about the different ways in which she has sought help with the issues she is facing in her life. She has been fascinated by the many gods of her Hindu meditation guide. She is learning that each expresses something of the mystery, beauty and power present naturally in the world. She has also been discussing what the 'power of God' means with her minister, especially as she comes to terms with terminal illness – or at least an illness the doctors say they can only 'manage' not cure. Her African prayer leader assures her that 'our God is a wonder-working God' – and she often comes away from these sessions feeling better physically and spiritually, feeling that she has been heard by God.

As Flora's situation demonstrates, practices involved in the giving and receiving of care are embedded in and arise out of the beliefs and values of the people who engage in them. Societal and cultural factors influence the shape and form of all caring activities. Flora's minister spends most of their time together in conversation and counselling, exploring her personal, inter-personal and family experiences. With the Asian woman she experiences physical release through the exercises and postures of *Hathayoga* and a deep inner calmness through meditation. With the African prayer leader she is moved by forms of prayer, ritual baths and spiritual exercises such as fasting, which reflect African cultures and spirituality. Flora recognizes and values the differing approaches to her manifold problems that are undertaken from different cultural and faith traditions. Caring acts are culture bound and the rationale of such acts is equally influenced by cultural and social considerations.

The art of pastoral theology explores the rationale, nature and ethos of care, as practised by and through communities of faith. Pastoral theology, which is by its very nature reflective practice, can be found in the various caring activities of persons and communities. Communities of faith have long sought to express their concern for the wellbeing of persons through reflective activities of love and service. Sermons, exhortations, counselling and other educational activities have often been the avenues through which persons have been encouraged, inspired and given the reason as well as the appropriate means to serve the welfare of people. Although the term has not always been used, 'pastoral theology' has been an essential part of attempts by faith communities to embody, 'enflesh' and refine the acts of love and care they engage in as an expression of their faith. As communities have faced particular traumas and tragedies, pastors and other care-givers have tried to find the best ways of helping people with their personal and communal needs. In the midst of pressing tasks of providing relief and care, they have tried to think what might be the best they can do in the light both of the need and of their faith.

In this book I attempt to articulate the nature of pastoral theology as clearly and distinctly as I can from the perspective of Christian faith. My objective is to help in the refining of caring activities through providing a critical assessment of both practice and theory. While reflection on and refining of caring practices is not new, the preparation and production of texts setting this out from particular faith perspectives has not been as forthcoming as might be desired. There are numerous reasons for the dearth of material in this field of theological activity, in spite of its age-long practice. Among them is the illusive and often highly personal nature of pastoral theology. Different practitioners approach and undertake their pastoral theological reflections and activities in very different ways. Another reason lies in the tendency among practitioners of care to emphasize the practice of it over against the theoretical aspects of their practice. Pastoral practitioners tend to 'get on with it' rather than philosophize or theorize about it.

Given widespread negative connotations associated with the term 'theology' in several places, especially in many western European contexts (for example, that it is the concern of a few esoteric, elitist and ivory-tower-encased professors, or else a few arcane clergy; that it has little to do with real life; that it has more to do with head than heart, with outdated books than current painful living), practitioners of the difficult yet crucial tasks of caring for people struggling with the messiness of life have often not been inclined to devote much of their precious time to theology and even less to producing tomes about it. It is also the case that the practical disciplines across the board, but especially in the arts and humanities, have tended to be less valued in western academies than the more abstract and theoretical. These reasons combine to make the production of books on pastoral theology unattractive. They, of course, rightly or wrongly, make particular assumptions about the nature both of 'pastoral' activity and of 'theology'.

The task and purpose of this book is to explore the following questions: What do we mean by 'pastoral theology'? What does it entail? Of what use is it and to whom? How do we understand it and how do we engage in it? This book is an attempt to provide an explanation of this form of theological activity by giving some clarity to the term. Its main purpose is to provide an introduction to the study and practice of pastoral theology. It aims at rendering the subject accessible to many people who are engaged in caring activities as well as those who would like to understand what is involved in care at the levels of both reflection and action. However, valuing as it does both theory and practice, this book goes beyond being merely programmatic. It does not reduce the subject to a list of techniques with reasons associated with them. It seeks to engage both theoretician and practitioner and to encourage a creative dialogue between them.

This book is written in such a way as to make the material available to and usable by a wide range of professional, amateur, lay and ordained reflective-practitioners at work in different settings. It is written by a practising Christian minister who has lived and worked on three continents and been influenced by ecumenical, interfaith and intercultural experiences over many years.

This is an introductory text. It invites readers to begin with the basic elements of pastoral theology, but it does not leave them there. Rather, readers are challenged to go further, to engage more deeply with the subject matter. Readers new to the subject will find basic information here. More experienced pastoral practitioners will find material that stimulates and challenges them to dig deeper in the reflective and expressive practices of pastoral theology. Different approaches are discussed. However, there is recognition and articulation of an underlying ethos. This ethos defines and constitutes the discipline of pastoral theology. This, then, is a book for practitioners of pastoral care in its many forms who are reflective about their practices.

Four important premises underlie this book and as such are in evidence throughout it. They are:

1   Pastoral theology is essentially *theology*, deeply concerned about the nature of God and the relationship between humanity and the divine.
2   Pastoral theology as theology is rooted in and tested by pastoral practice.
3   There is an underlying ethos that distinguishes pastoral

theology from other theological disciplines and provides both rhyme and reason for the discipline.

4 We all live in a multicultural world and are influenced and informed by many different social forces.

I shall be arguing that theology is not merely about doctrines and propositions but is also about how we understand and live in the world as it is. At its heart, theology has to do with an exploration of how we understand and experience God as well as what is ultimately real and true in essence about the world. Another way of saying this is to claim that theology offers views about what really is. An affirmation that God is Creator of all things is a statement that points both to the nature of God and to the ultimate nature of reality. 'God is originator and source of all' is an affirmation of the ultimate essence of all things. Part of the task of theology is to assist our understanding of both God and reality from the perspective of God's presence and activity in the world. I take it that truth is one in God and that God is related to the whole of reality. Consequently nothing that is true about the world is unrelated to God. Thus to say, for example, that God is Trinity is to suggest that reality is itself in some sense communal and relational. A theological exploration is therefore a quest to understand what is true about God and the nature of the world.

This book is written by an African Christian who has been shaped and formed by the western Christian tradition, especially the Methodist experience and interpretation of it, in its various global expressions. My African heritage constitutes the root of my existence. I was born and raised in Ghana and greatly cherish the rich traditions and culture bequeathed to me there by my forebears. My Christian heritage has provided the wings for my journey in life. This heritage has influenced me to value not only the richness of the Christian tradition but also that which John Wesley described as its 'catholic spirit'. That is to say that there is something of worldwide significance in this way of understanding God and the world.

6

As such what is sought is a global dialogue in which many may participate. This self-consciously ecumenical posture seeks to articulate ideas that various sections of the Christian Church might find valuable in their work. My dual African and Christian heritages continually challenge and encourage me on the journey of life.

I have been nurtured, stimulated and challenged through being a part, for most of my life, of ecumenical as well as secular institutions in West Africa, Britain, Europe and North America. My thinking has also been shaped and influenced by experiences of traditions and peoples of different faith professions. I hope, therefore, that beyond the Christian Church, persons of different religious and other traditions, who wish to be intentional and reflective about their practices of care, find this book useful. Lifelong involvement in interfaith dialogue and interaction has certainly greatly enriched my life on both a personal and professional level.

The overriding purpose of my writing in this respect is to enable pastoral practitioners of different faith traditions to hone their reflective and expressive skills and thus to engage more fully in theologically informed practice as well as theology that is influenced, grounded and shaped by practice. I write out of my own African Christian tradition to emphasize the fact that it is not necessary to abandon one's heritage in order to be ecumenical. Interfaith dialogue presupposes religious integrity on the part of those who participate in the dialogue. Dialogue is not advanced by a mushy sentimentality that seeks to obliterate any differences between participants. There can be no dialogue without the owning of distinct and clear positions. Nevertheless, dialogue is also premised upon respect and understanding. Participants need to pursue an ethic of non-violence, openness to learning and a preparedness to be self-critical. These have been the values that have shaped my own life and are ones I wish to share.

This book was originally conceived and constructed under the title *Groundwork of Pastoral Theology*. When I was first invited to write it in 1997, I was a lecturer at the University of

Birmingham in Britain – a secular university with a Department of Theology endowed with a Chair by the distinguished Birmingham Cadbury family, whose religious heritage is Quaker. Having studied for and completed my doctorate in theology at that institution in 1984, I returned to my native land of Ghana in West Africa where for five years I taught seminary students from many different Protestant traditions, and other university students, the theories and practices of pastoral care and counselling. In 1989 I returned to my alma mater in Britain where, among other things, I taught students from many different parts of the world enrolled on a master's programme in pastoral studies. Following 12 years of lecturing in Britain, I moved to the United States of America. I find myself writing these words from Candler School of Theology at Emory University in Atlanta, Georgia, deep in the South of the USA. Immediately prior to taking up my current position at Candler, I was for three years engaged in the task of teaching and preparing pastors to serve churches primarily within the Presbyterian Church, USA, at Columbia Theological Seminary, Decatur, Georgia. Ecumenicity, intercultural and international relations summarize very much the experience and context out of which this book is written.

Crossing boundaries and helping others do so has been the main activity of much of my professional life and ministry. Over the years I have gained the conceptual framework and the philosophical apparatus to understand cultural and systemic differences. Nevertheless, culture shocks continue to be an inevitable part of my experience. No amount of intellectual preparation or visiting can fully prepare one for living in a different culture. Cognitive abilities alone are insufficient to navigate the deep waters of cultural and national difference. Emotional and spiritual intelligence are also required. Following years of transitioning into new social, cultural and national environments I have observed a pattern which I summarize in four phases.

Phase 1 Encountering the system. In this initial phase, also described as that of culture shock, the stranger comes

INTRODUCTION

into contact with the full force of the different system. The stranger's life is characterized by feelings of confusion, rejection, frequent physical ailments, helplessness, bewilderment, being an outsider, and a longing to be 'normal', ordinary, to blend in.

Phase 2 Understanding the system. Here the stranger begins to gain a better cognitive understanding of the educational, cultural and linguistic practices and customs of the hosts. There is a decided shift from the vulnerability and emotionality of the first phase to being a little bit more in control. They begin to deal more adequately with expectations of themselves as well as others. They increase in ability to recognize and navigate real differences and perceive similarities with what they were familiar with elsewhere.

Phase 3 Living within the system. In this phase, cognitive and emotional responses begin to cohere and greater familiarity with the system occurs, together with a heightened ability to live more normally within the new system. The stranger begins to participate more fully in the customs and rituals of the culture. Participation in sports and supporting the local teams has been crucial for me in this regard. Being known and recognized, even if only vicariously as a result of the sporting abilities of one's children, can be a real breath of fresh air.

Phase 4 Having (and using) authority within the system. Finally one begins to be able to explain how things work to others with an understanding of it oneself. One begins to appreciate the reasons for the 'contradictions' and challenges within the system. This leads to the confidence to insist on one's rights and to assume one's responsibilities within the system.

The dilemma that I have encountered frequently throughout my professional life – and that continues to be present in the writing of this book – is one of how appropriately to address the likely audience of any piece of my writing. I am keenly aware

9

of the importance of cultural context. I have come, through personal and professional work in different countries, to see just how deeply and pervasively cultural and social transmission affects us all. What makes immediate sense to an audience in one cultural context may leave an audience in another context cold. Like jokes, the best of which are untranslatable, what is declared with confidence to one audience may be of absolutely no consequence to another in a different country. How does one address different audiences in one medium with integrity? I find that there are things to be said in Britain that Americans would not say or relate to. Similarly there are issues that Americans in the South would find relevant that would make little sense to people in Britain. Add to that what is of importance to Ghanaians, other West Africans, Diasporan Africans, Latin Americans, Asians, Australians and Pacific Islanders, and you realize that the task begins to assume complexities that only a simpleton would ignore. How does one give voice to the concerns and interests of West Africans in ways that would communicate with them as well as with Europeans and Americans? How does one respect views that are considered, on a dominant scheme of thought, underdeveloped, which on another scheme are highly valued? The response of one of my dialogue partners is simply that one cannot 'be all things to all people' and as such one should not even try to be. His solution to this dilemma is that one should only speak of one's own reality to a specific, clearly defined audience, preferably of one's own people. This is helpful only to the extent that it heightens the dilemma for me. The point is that my own reality has been shaped and influenced by multiple cultures and traditions. To that extent my own reality is itself pluriform. My 'own people' are a whole bunch – and diverse to the core.

Another significant aspect of this dilemma lies in the fact that what is written in the West, and in the disciplines of pastoral theology, care and counselling in particular, invariably ends up informing and shaping the practices of pastoral care and counselling around the world. As a result, if what is written here remains insensitive to, or else uninformed by, other than a western perspective, then what is learned and practised globally will continue to be western in nature and content. To that extent the rich practices and thoughts of peoples around the globe in the religious and reflective practices of pastoral care and counselling will remain local knowledge that does not influence the theoretical development of these disciplines.

The way in which I have chosen to respond to this dilemma in this book is to attempt to adopt what I have elsewhere described as an intercultural approach.[1] In this approach, seriousness is attached, among others, to three principles: contextuality, multiple perspectives and authentic participation. Context has a highly significant influence upon behaviour and belief. As such, behaviours and beliefs need to be understood and analysed within their context. To expect sameness in response to issues from different contexts is to lose sight of the strength of this influence. Much will be made of the social, cultural and historic context of the sources upon which I draw. In doing so I must face the reality that others from other contexts might disagree very strongly with some of the affirmations arising out of different contexts. What is realistic is the recognition and affirmation of multiple – indeed conflicting – perspectives. I acknowledge within myself as well as with others the existence of many different perspectives on most issues. I am called upon to name the perspectives and to explore how they may be related to context. With this polyphonic approach I am also called upon to respect the rationality and integrity of those who hold differing views on the same issues. Such naming and respect includes the need for authentic participation in which many, from different backgrounds and of differing viewpoints, are admitted to the table on their own grounds. In this book, then, an attempt is made to approach the issues interculturally, respecting context, expecting difference of perspective and allowing many, including conflicting, voices to be heard.

In this way my hope is that many more voices will have

influence on the shaping of theory and practice in the disciplines under study. Thus pastoral theology begins to be more reflective of the plurality within the world. Moreover, practitioners and teachers of the disciplines in the West will have a wider and deeper knowledge of the global context and thus be more sensitive to, and help students be more informed about, the global contexts in which we all now live and work.

The book begins in Chapter 1 with an exploration of the nature of the discipline of pastoral theology. What do we mean by the term? What kind of activity is it? What sources does it draw upon and why does it use particular resources? What are the limits or boundaries of the subject? In Chapter 1, then, the nature and character of pastoral theology is established and some boundaries are indicated that should enable us more clearly to characterize and recognize pastoral theology.

All pastoral theology, and indeed all theology, arises out of specific historical, geographical, socio-political, economic and cultural contexts. In recognition of this fact, Chapter 2 is given over to contextual considerations. By reflecting on developments and practices in pastoral care and counselling in different regions of the world, this chapter demonstrates the contextual nature of pastoral theology. The influence of context on evident preferences and approaches is illustrated. In this chapter the global as well as the local nature of pastoral theology becomes evident. The global phenomena of pastoral theology are manifest in the very fact of distinct local concerns and different approaches arising out of differing contexts.

Much of what happens in any discipline is the result of how people go about producing and developing it. As such, Chapter 3 discusses issues of method, setting out a range of different methodologies and approaches adopted in the processes and practices of pastoral theology. This chapter helps us understand how pastoral theology is generated and offers us tools for the production as well as the critique of this theological enterprise.

Pastoral theology qua *theology* seeks to make contributions to the articulation of faith concerning the nature of God. In line with this, Chapter 4 deals with the content of pastoral theology. This chapter explores contributions to an understanding of the nature of God and of Christian faith that have arisen out of the reflective practice of pastoral care in different settings. A central argument of the book is made clear here. It is that pastoral theology *is* theology – not simply rationale for technique, nor again merely 'application' of theory: pastoral theology is theology in essence and not merely derivative of or parasitic upon 'real' theology.

The final chapter (Chapter 5) attempts to make explicit some of the ways in which pastoral theology may render a service to, and be in interaction with, other disciplines of theology. It explores pastoral theological interactions within different communities and institutions in different parts of the world. This is in recognition of the interdisciplinary nature of pastoral theology and the ways in which it has been enriched through dialogue with other human sciences. It also recognizes the relevance of the methods of pastoral theology to the social, cultural, religious and political spheres of our common life throughout the world.

The Nature of Pastoral Theology

Pastoral theology as reflective action

Pastoral theology is reflective activity that brings together action and reflection in dialogically and mutually critical ways. An initial definition of pastoral theology would see it as *reflection on the caring activities of God and human communities*. Pastoral theologians are attentive to the accounts that faith communities give, record and recount concerning their experiences and beliefs about the ways in which God cares. They also pay attention to the caring activities that human communities engage in and ask questions about how these are influenced by, and also influence, their faith. Pastoral theologians commit themselves to engage in particular forms of reflection that have the characteristics of being critical, constructive, interpretive and expressive. Pastoral theology, then, entails *critical, interpretive, constructive and expressive reflection on the caring activities of God and human communities*.

Critical and constructive

The 'critical and constructive' nature of pastoral theology has been explored in the important text, *Foundations for a Practical Theology of Ministry* by James Poling and Donald Miller (1985). By 'critical' Poling and Miller helpfully refer to a number of features. First, being critical means having some knowledge about and being able to engage in the analytical methods of 'socio-historical research' (p. 62). Second, being critical entails being self-reflexive. It means 'continuous self-criticism to become aware of the biases, assumptions, and self-interests' that have an impact on persons' views. Third, to be critical means to have 'a method of exploring [the] conceptual bias that results from socio-economic, political and psychological' influences (p. 63). Being 'constructive' involves seeking affirmations and assessments that are both descriptive and normative, expressing views both on what is and what ought to be. Constructive reflection is creative. One who engages in this form of reflection is prepared to propose ideas that are related to and based on existing knowledge, but that takes such knowledge in new and innovative directions. In line with this way of thinking the 'critical and constructive' in our definition refer to the processes and methods of analysis, self-critical reflection and creative construction that contribute to theological study.

Interpretive

The 'interpretive' involves, as Farley puts it, 'thinking of situations under Gospel' (Farley, 2003, p. 8). Farley's account of theology in this regard is instructive. 'Theology', he argues, 'is an interpretive or thinking activity determined by Gospel, the concern for truth, and a response to the present situation' (p. 7). Like Farley, I believe that a primary and constitutive form of any theological exercise is interpretation. One of faith's most basic functions lies in interpreting and seeking understanding of situations in the light of faith's essential frame of reference. As such, pastoral theology throws the light of the gospel on the situations and circumstances of human life and seeks to understand and act in response to these situations in the light of this interpretation. For liberation theologians Leonardo Boff and Clodovis Boff, 'there is such a thing as pastoral theology: it is the theology that sheds the light of the saving word on the reality of injustice so as to inspire the church to struggle for liberation' (1987, p. 17), and the objective is the 'liberating practice of love' (p. 17). Acts, activities, contexts, situations and texts are all subjected to the interpretation of the gospel in this theological endeavour. In pastoral theology, caring activities of various kinds are interpreted, illuminated and critiqued in the light of the gospel.

Interpretation also opens the way for further dialogue between disciplines and traditions. In this regard, Charles Gerkin's usage of a hermeneutical mode in re-visioning pastoral counselling is a significant theological insight (Gerkin, 1984). Gerkin sees pastoral counselling as basically an interpretive practice by means of which persons are enabled to find meaning and narrative sense in their lives. For him pastoral counselling is 'a process of interpretation and re-interpretation of human experience within the framework of a primary orientation toward the Christian mode of interpretation in dialogue with contemporary psychological modes of interpretation'. Thus 'the most basic tools of pastoral counselling are therefore seen as hermeneutical tools – the tools of interpretation' (Gerkin, 1984, p. 21).

Expressive

The expressive nature of pastoral theology refers to the many ways in which pastoral theological activity is made manifest through art, music, liturgy, sermon, counselling, pastoral care and acts of service. These forms of practice are expressive of particular interpretive and constructive activities essential to pastoral theological reflection and practice. Whenever a funeral service is planned, for example, various elements are brought together in an attempt to remember and honour the dead while also caring for the bereaved. The music is chosen to reflect the life of the deceased. Hymns and, increasingly, secular songs that the departed (or the mourners) love feature on the programme. Photographs expressive of the life of the one we mourn are displayed. The homily at best reflects the deceased's life story and seeks points of interaction with the stories of Christian faith. The whole tapestry of the liturgical event is woven out of the stuff of the person's life as it interacts with our common human life story. In all of this, sight is not lost of the bereaved community and connections are made to enable them to grieve and then gently to move on. A funeral service, when handled carefully, is an instance of what we are calling expressive pastoral theology.

Human and divine

While pastoral theology is clearly a human endeavour, there are at least two poles in this definition, each of which is necessary for the discipline. There is, on the one hand, what might be called the divine or 'God' dimension, and there is, on the other hand, the 'human' dimension or component. The God dimension includes notions (doctrines, views, teachings, perceptions etc.) as well as experiences of God. Pastoral theologians, to greater or lesser degrees, assume that God is an active, loving and caring presence discernible by human persons in the world, both in history and today. God is seen as being related in important ways to the life of persons and communities. Further, God's reality and presence, discernible by human persons, by no means completely subsumes the nature of God. There will always be unknown and essentially unknowable aspects of the 'God' dimension. The term 'God' refers inevitably to mystery and that which lies beyond human grasp. As such, pastoral theologians bring to their art exegetical, hermeneutical and experiential explorations of the nature of God and of faith, always conscious of the fact that there are aspects of the mystery of God that lie outside of and beyond human grasp. Included in this is the Christian sense that in some way God wishes to be known and so does find ways in which to reveal what is knowable about God to humankind.

The 'human' dimension is approached here through communities, to highlight the importance of both corporate and personal aspects of the human situation. Humans are communal creatures formed and shaped in community. Human care, even when it is practised by and with individuals, is set within communities of faith, practice and culture. Thus, any examination of the caring activities of human communities necessarily includes individual, interpersonal and communal aspects. Human reflection and activity are set within communal structures.

Focus on care

The main focus of pastoral theology is on care and caring activity. As such, the reflective and expressive activities of pastoral theology focus on the care-giving activities of God and of human communities. Moreover, in pastoral theology the divine and the human poles are held together in interactive tension. Both poles are seen as crucial. It is necessary to explore the caring activity of God as experienced and expressed in history. It is important also to examine the rich variety of caring activities that human communities engage in. The interaction between these two is a site of both revelatory knowledge and discernment. Something can be known about both the divine and the human through an examination of the caring activities of human communities. Part of the craft of pastoral theology is to explore and critically discern what may be of theological significance in all caring activities. It is also the task of this discipline to examine and refine caring practice by paying close attention to theologies that may be implied or else explicitly expressed in the practices by which communities define themselves and by which they seek to express their faith or culture.

Characteristics of pastoral theology

In the very useful *Blackwell Reader in Pastoral and Practical Theology* (Woodward and Pattison (eds), 2000, pp. 13–16), editors James Woodward and Stephen Pattison outline as many as 14 'essential characteristics' of 'practical theology' (used interchangeably with 'pastoral theology' in their book). They argue that practical theology is not satisfied simply to end in an aesthetic statement but rather is *transformational*, aiming to make some difference in people's understanding and actual life situation. Practical theology is not only concerned with propositions and logic but also finds place for human emotions, the *symbolic* and even the 'irrational' in addressing all of human experience. Practical theology, according to Woodward and Pattison, is also *confessional* and *honest* in that it is committed to facing up to the importance and relevance of religious experience in the contemporary world. Practical theologians avoid merely abstract considerations of real life experiences of pain and suffering – such as childhood cancer – and rather seek to find better ways of thinking about and responding to such situations.

In a direct play on words and concepts, Woodward and Pattison describe practical theology as *unsystematic*. Their point is that in contrast to some traditional kinds of theology that have claimed universal validity and completeness, practical theology is always 'provisional and flexible'. 'Because it continuously has to re-engage with the fragmented realities and changes of the contemporary world and the issues it presents, much practical theology is not systematic or complete' (p. 14). Practical theologians are called upon to be *truthful* and *committed*, keeping faith with the reality, complexity and messiness of much of life. Practical theologians cannot gloss over awkward or untidy aspects of human life. Moreover, in practical theology priority is given to context or situation – a point which will be elaborated in Chapter 2 of this book. Practical theology is *contextual and situationally related* in both diagnosis and prescription. Attention to the context and situation-in-life of persons is a crucial aspect of the pastoral theologian's craft. As a result it is *socio-politically aware and committed*, with an awareness of and orientation to the challenges presented to both theory and practice by social and political movements.

Pastoral theology is *experiential* not only because it takes people's experiences very seriously but precisely because these experiences are taken as 'data for theological reflection, analysis and thought' (p. 15). I would extend that by saying, as

Seward Hiltner argued in the 1950s, that people's experiences when reflected upon can also be theologically revelatory. In other words, we learn something about the nature of God through reflection on people's experiences. Pastoral theology then arises out of reflection on the experiences and responses of human communities. As Hiltner writes:

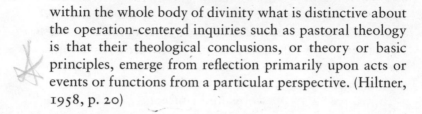

> within the whole body of divinity what is distinctive about the operation-centered inquiries such as pastoral theology is that their theological conclusions, or theory or basic principles, emerge from reflection primarily upon acts or events or functions from a particular perspective. (Hiltner, 1958, p. 20)

Practical theology, as presented by Woodward and Pattison, is *interrogative*, asking pertinent and incisive questions about the nature of God, reality and practice. In addition it is *dialectical* and *disciplined*. In saying this they draw attention to practical theology's activity of holding polarities in creative tension. As I also argue, pastoral theologians practise the art of maintaining dialectic and creative tension between theory and practice, tradition and experience, the real and the ideal, the literary and the non-literary, different disciplines, the sacred and the secular. Woodward and Pattison point to practical and pastoral theology as a field, and the numerous essays in their volume give eloquent testimony to this fact, which is a diverse and developing one 'that can be both exciting and confusing in equal measure for the newcomer' (p. 16).

Creative tension

Crucial to an understanding of pastoral theology, then, is the insistence that the critical, interpretive, constructive and expressive dimensions be held together in creative tension. The expressive is not merely an application of the critical and constructive. In reality, construction and critique are as much a part of the expressive as the expressive is of the constructive and critical, and each is interpretive in nature. Pastoral theology entails the art and craft of maintaining the mutual interaction between the critical, interpretive, constructive and expressive abilities of persons in communities of faith, practice and culture. This interaction is premised upon recognition of the equal value and importance in the pastoral theological task of the critical, the interpretive, the constructive and the expressive activities of communities of faith, practice and culture. Pastoral theologians are motivated by an integrative impulse to keep these different forms of activity informing and influencing each other.

Pastoral theology as performative craft

Pastoral theology is perhaps best conceived of as both an interpretive and a performative craft. Illustrating the usefulness of considering biblical interpretation as akin to the art of performing a musical piece on an instrument, Frances Young in *The Art of Performance* (1990) offers an enlightening approach to Scripture that bridges gaps between the academic and the pastoral. She argues:

> The Biblical Canon, then, is as it were the repertoire, inherited, given, to be performed. Selections are performed day by day and week by week in the liturgy. Exegetes, like musicians, need the discipline of rehearsing the score, trying out ways of interpretation, researching the possibilities of meaning, grappling with the 'physical' or 'historical' constraints of the language, preparing for performance with appropriate ornamentation. (p. 25)

Following the analogy of artistic performance, pastoral theology can be seen as an art that seeks to uncover and communicate the beauty of God and the creation in the face of experiences and situations that would deny both. Gordon Jackson makes a similar point as he draws on insights from process theology in presenting ministry as being about 'creating something of beauty'. Jackson writes:

> Each of us is summoned by the creative God at work in the world to work with the divine Artist . . . to create something of beauty as we process through our days and years empowered by the creative love of God to bring healing to our communal life. (Jackson, 1998, p. xvi)

The idea of pastoral theology as craft is highly evocative. A craft entails a skill that is learned, most often through apprenticeship, and that is geared towards an aesthetically pleasing product. The picture then is of the pastoral theologian as a person who has been formed, who in turn forms, creates, shapes or interacts with the things around her or him in ways that result in the coming into being of objects of beauty.

The form of pastoral theology: practice or theory?

> *Arjuna*: You speak so highly of the renunciation of action; yet you ask me to follow the yoga of action. Now tell me definitely: which of these is better?

> *Sri Krishna*: . . . The yoga of action, say the ignorant, is different from the yoga of the knowledge of Brahman.
> The wise see knowledge and action as one:
> They see truly.
> Take either path
> And tread it to the end:
> The end is the same.
> There followers of action
> Meet seekers after knowledge
> In equal freedom.

> (The Yoga of Renunciation, *Bhagavad-Gita*, 69–70)

In recent years, discussions of theology by systematic as well as practical theologians have sought to return to an insistence that theology is a practical discipline (for example, Browning, 1996; Volf and Bass, 2002; Farley, 2003). By reference to practical theology and its historical nature, Farley argues that viewing theology as practical wisdom for living goes as far back as Scottish theologian and philosopher John Duns Scotus (1266–1308).

> Widespread from the Middle Ages through the seventeenth century is the view that 'theology' names a *habitus* or disposition of the soul. The prevailing view among Protestant, Reformed and Lutheran theologians was that this *habitus* and its knowledge were of the practical and not just theoretical kind. Theology is, accordingly a practical knowledge having the character of wisdom since its object is God and the things of God grasped in the situation of faith and salvation. (Farley, 2003, p. 169)

The idea of theology as practical wisdom for living is related to notions of *habitus*, a way of thinking that is linked with Aristotelian notions of *phronesis* (practical good sense). *Habitus* (habit) refers to an orientation or way of being disposed toward things. Sociologist Pierre Bourdieu has elaborated and nuanced the notion of *habitus* so that the implied practice is seen in terms of structures, strategies and cultural products (Bourdieu, 1990, pp. 52–65). Christian theology, in this renewed thinking that seeks to reconnect it with the age-old concept of theology as *habitus*, is seen as related to the life of the Church and to the life and faith of Christian people. Christian theology in this sense is the articulation of the nature and understanding of the Christian faith as it undergirds and is expressed through practical living.

The discipline of practical theology has often been seen in academic circles as involving the articulation in word and deed of the theoretical bases of the practices by which Christian faith is constituted and enacted. Although this way of thinking about practical theology is widespread outside the guilds of practical and pastoral theology, it is recognized within them as severely inadequate. The reason for this is that this way of thinking unfortunately tends to collapse an important tension between two poles. Theological work is seen on this view exclusively as the theoretical part of the enterprise. As such, pastoral theology becomes the form of practical theology that provides the theory for pastoral care. Pastoral theology, then, is the theory undergirding the practice of pastoral care. When this collapsing of the necessary tension between theory and practice happens, the crucial nature of the discipline is lost and it ceases to make the significant contribution that is needed within theological studies.

Pastoral theology as praxis

Pastoral theology does not resolve the creative tension between practice and theory into the one dimension of the theoretical or reflective. Instead, pastoral theology is properly a dialectical discipline. Pastoral theology considers itself as crucially engaged in the mutual critique involved in the tension between theory and practice. Pastoral theology is a 'praxeological' discipline – one in which practical action and theory are held together in critical and creative tension. Here, theory critiques action and action critiques theory. Stephen Bevans, with reference to the thinking of Karl Marx, Paulo Freire and Philip Berryman, captures the meaning of this most clearly in his discussion of the 'praxis model' of contextual theology. 'Praxis' is not simply a faddish expression for 'practice'. Bevans helpfully explains that praxis is 'reflected-upon action and acted-upon reflection – both rolled into one' (Bevans, 2002, p. 72). Bevans writes:

> When we speak of the praxis model of contextual theology, we are speaking about a model the central insight of which is that theology is done not simply by providing relevant expressions of Christian faith but also by commitment to Christian action. But even more than this, theology is understood as the product of the continual dialogue of these two aspects of Christian life. (p. 72)

Theory provides rationale and method for practice. Practice shapes, informs and offers critical tools for theory. These two are not separated off into isolated disciplines or activities but rather are held together in creative and critical tension. American theologian David Tracy (1975) makes this abundantly clear when he writes that '*praxis* is correctly understood as the critical relationship between theory and practice whereby each is dialectically influenced and transformed by the other' (p. 243). Pastoral theologians are reflective practitioners whose theology and action are so closely intertwined and mutually critical as to be separable only for the purposes of discussion.

Pastoral theology as Practical Divinity

Taking an example from the tradition in Christianity that has been most influential in my own formation, this, to my mind, lies at the heart of the way in which John Wesley, founding father of worldwide Methodism, conceived of theology. Wesley referred to theology as *Practical Divinity*. As Thomas Langford and others have argued, 'Wesley's theology . . . is practical in nature and intention. It grew out of practice, was a reflection upon practice and aimed to enhance practice. It was for the shaping of life and he rightly called it "Practical Divinity"' (Langford, 1998b, p. 3).

John Wesley understood theology as essentially a practical discipline in which theory and practice could not be separated but rather each affected the other. Theological understanding in this way of reckoning is for the purpose of guiding Christian existence, and Christian existence informs and shapes theological interpretation.

Pastoral theology, then, takes both 'life' (that is, action, practice) and 'faith' (that is, theory, reflection) seriously. Each deserves careful study. One distinctive and indeed constitutive characteristic of pastoral theology lies in the fact that it seeks to enable these two spheres to interact in mutually critical, constructive and expressive ways. It is this crucial activity of facilitating the maintenance of the tension between these spheres of human activity that provides an important distinguishing feature of the discipline of pastoral theology.

The clerical paradigm

In a well-researched and carefully referenced book, Thomas Oden (1983) presents pastoral theology as dealing with the office and functions of the ordained pastor. Oden's approach in this work is firmly within a longstanding tradition regarding the meaning of 'pastoral', namely that it essentially refers to that which pertains to the work or role of the 'ordained Christian pastor'. As Farley has shown, this conception and formulation, which Farley terms the 'clerical paradigm', was concretized in the nineteenth century (see Farley, 1987). Oden usefully seeks to connect pastoral practices – preaching, worship and teaching – with the historical, doctrinal and ecclesiastical disciplines of the wider theological curriculum. This approach is useful for focus and in-depth study of the role of the ordained pastor. Its historical focus on the first five centuries of the Christian era enables the pastoral theologian to be rooted in Christian history and tradition and to see the practices of ministry in relation to this tradition.

However, the clerical paradigm narrows the pastoral activity too sharply. It restricts ministry to individual agency and so misses out on the rich opportunity to study the communitarian nature of Christian ministry. Moreover, it gives little or no attention to the influence of practice upon theory down through the years of Christian ministry. Instead of paying attention to Christian practices it restricts itself to the person and activity of the clergyman or woman. This criticism of the clerical paradigm lies at the heart of a more comprehensive understanding of pastoral theology traceable in the works of Catholic theologian Karl Rahner, Ed Farley and of several other British, European and US theologians (for example, see Rahner and Schuster, 1965; Farley, 1982; 2003; Lambourne, 1974; Wilson, 1988). Demonstrations of the inadequacies of the clerical paradigm are also clearly evident in the work of feminist, liberationist, postmodernist and post-colonialist theologians (Graham, 1996; Miller-McLemore and Gill-Austern, 1999; Lartey, 2003) who in different ways show how several important voices are ruled out by the focus of this paradigm.

Practices of communities

Narrowly conceived pastoral theology focuses on pastoral care and pastoral counselling. More broadly it encompasses all the practices through which practitioners of the Christian faith express their love of God and others, including preaching, prayer, worship and teaching. What is distinctive about 'pastoral' theology is its concern with 'practices of care' that may find expression through a number of different activities within the life of the Church and other human communities. Its concern is to relate these caring activities to God's caring as revealed and understood within the faith traditions, in critical and constructive ways. This emphasis on practice provides the key for pastoral theology in a postmodern 'age of uncertainty' as expounded by Elaine Graham (1996). Graham argues significantly:

> The proper focus of pastoral theology is not the pastoral agent, or theological ethics, or applied theology, but the pastoral *practice* of the faith-community itself. By focusing on the reality of practice, we are able to recognize that theory and practice do not exist independently. Metaphysical principles require concrete human agency. The arena of Christian *praxis* – value-directed and value-laden action – is understood as the medium through which the Christian community embodies and enacts its fundamental vision of the Gospel. (Graham, 1996, p. 7)

Graham's emphasis on Christian praxis, specifically the pastoral practice of the faith-community, correctly names the form of practical theology. Pastoral theology as we are identifying it examines as its primary focus all *practices of care* engaged in by communities of faith.

The scope of pastoral theology: how far does it go?

If pastoral theology studies the loving practices of care of Christian communities, and Christian faith encompasses love – which is expressed through care – then is all of Christian activity not a form of pastoral theology? What is it that specifies and distinguishes the *pastoral* discipline? It is necessary to clarify the scope of pastoral theology lest it be defined to include everything and so lose any meaningfulness as a distinct discipline.

Pastoral theologians may take as a starting point a study of the records in the Jewish and Christian Scriptures and other sacred writings of the caring presence and actions of God towards humanity. More usually pastoral theologians begin with a study of activities of care practised by Christian and other human communities that are engaged in as interactive with convictions that arise from faith.[2] It is those activities that imply notions of God's love in caring action that are its focus. Where human communities perceive themselves to be summoned and inspired by the love of God and neighbour to act in the care of persons, there pastoral theology finds a particular interest. Wherever the shape and form of practices of care are implicitly or explicitly influenced by models derived from traditions of faith, there again pastoral theologians find their work.

Pastoral theology, then, operates around and studies the central themes of *faith-inspired care* and *care-inspired faith*. Pastoral theologians focus on studying 'care' and 'faith' and the interrelationships between them. This focus de-limits the activity of pastoral theology and offers an essential character and scope to the discipline. However, it is important to emphasize that notions of individual care or the care of individuals in distress do by no means exhaust the subject of care being referred to here. In the rapidly changing social, economic, cultural and political climate evident in different parts of the world, it is imperative that care is understood not in a paternalistic, doing-good-to-needy-others fashion but rather in a variety of ways, including empowerment, facilitating, support, nurture and liberation with and for persons and communities.[3]

In order for pastoral theologians to engage in a genuinely relevant exercise in the current social, cultural, religious and political climate in the world, any discussion of practices of care has to explore the global situation. The scope of pastoral theology in the twenty-first century has to lie beyond the confines of the geographical boundaries of Europe, the United Kingdom and the United States. The scope has to be what is now described as the 'global village'. A changing socio-economic, political, cultural and religious climate necessitates taking contexts outside of the West far more seriously than ever before. In point of fact this is also necessary even if Britain and the United States were our only focus. Pluralism and multiculturalism are such facts of life in the West that it is unthinkable that Graham's comment to the effect that 'the implications of ethnic, cultural and racial diversity are under-developed in contemporary pastoral literature' (Graham, 1996, p. 47) continues to be the case. As such, in this book global developments and trends in pastoral care are given consideration. This is to say that no serious pastoral theologian can ignore what is happening in any part of the world as if it had nothing to do with them. What happens in the mountains of Afghanistan and Pakistan may have crucial importance for the care of persons in New York, London, Nairobi and Dar-es-Salaam. The atrocities of suicide with mass murder on 11 September 2001 in the United States, 11 March 2004 in Madrid, Spain, in July 2005 in London, in Malaysia and in other places, undertaken ostensibly under the inspiration of religious sentiments, bear eloquent testimony to the need for this. Presumably religions that espouse peace and love may inspire some of their practitioners to undertake acts of violence to themselves and others as a manifestation of their care and concern for the world situation.

It is my contention that basic to the scope of pastoral theology is a requirement to include in its study and practice all that has to do with the care of persons and communities within the global village. The geographical scope of pastoral theology needs to be *global* following the God 'who so loved *the world* that he gave his Son' (John 3.16).

Sources of pastoral theology

One of the generally acknowledged sources of all forms of theology is Scripture. Indeed the life and practice of many religious communities is shaped by the ways in which their Scriptures are received and interpreted. Although he never used the term, Wesley's theological method has been described as involving a 'quadrilateral' of standards, sources or principles, namely Scripture, reason, experience and tradition. In this Wesley epitomizes generally acknowledged sources of many traditions of Christian theology. According to Maddox, Wesley did use each one of these four criteria in his theological judgements. However, Maddox argues that his most usual way of authenticating a position as Christian was to assert that it was 'both scriptural and rational' or that it was 'scriptural and in accord with tradition' (Maddox, 1994, p. 36). Wesley customarily referred to at least two of the four sources of authority identified in the quadrilateral. Notably, in all cases one of the two would be Scripture. It is important that this practical theologian of an earlier age reserved such a significant place for Scripture.

Scripture

Christian theologians have continued, to varying degrees, to consistently identify the Bible as a crucial source of authority for determining Christian belief and practice. Scripture holds a significant place in all of Christian faith and theology. As such it does play an important role in pastoral theology. However, it is important to recognize that there are a myriad ways of approaching the Bible and that these are reflected in the ways in which pastoral theologians have dealt with it.

Some pastoral theologians read and interpret the Bible as the 'oracle of God' (McKnight, 2003, p. 2268). They take the Bible as unique and perfect, having divinely bestowed authority and revealing directly the will, purpose and nature of God. They go to Scripture not to dispute or discuss its context and relevance, but rather to hear 'the word of God'. The Bible is seen as possessing the answer to all the issues and woes faced by human persons. This devotional and often liturgical approach is by no means unthinking. However, it is subject to the dangers of biblicism in which the literal words, or else the book itself, are such sacred objects that they are taken literally and may become a legalistic battering ram used more to defeat than to inspire and encourage persons. A great danger is also present in the assumption that only literal, and not critical or contextual, readings and interpretations lead to hearing 'the word of God'. Some extremists have abused Scripture in just such a fashion.

British pastoral theologian Stephen Pattison identifies a 'tokenist' use of the Bible by some pastoral theologians (Pattison, 1993, pp. 120-1). This amounts to 'indiscriminate use of parts of Scripture to add an air of religious respectability or legitimation to theories or practices undertaken on other grounds' (p. 120). Although this approach acknowledges the importance of Scripture it fails precisely to give due weight to it, abusing it by never really going beyond face value. Instead, what such users of the Bible do is merely quote passages as a means to make what is done look good spiritually.

A more savoury approach utilized by pastoral theologians draws on imagery or analogies from Scripture that may have illuminative value for the task of caring. An engaging example of such usage can be found in Alastair Campbell's important book *Rediscovering Pastoral Care* (1981). Campbell employs the biblical images of the 'shepherd', the 'wounded healer' and the 'wise fool' to illustrate the nature and functions of pastoral care. Campbell utilizes these images in this way to articulate a pastoral theology. The image of shepherd of course has been the central biblical image that pastoral theologians have referred to down through the years. Seward Hiltner (1909–84), who perhaps did more than any single individual in the recent past to establish and foster pastoral theology as a serious academic and practical discipline, especially in the US, made this image the cornerstone of his understanding of the pastoral theologian's craft. In a seminal study of pastoral theology, Hiltner defined pastoral theology as 'that branch or field of theological knowledge and inquiry that brings the shepherding perspective to bear upon all the operations and functions of the church and the minister, and then draws conclusions of a theological order from reflections on these observations' (Hiltner, 1958, p. 20). The imagery of 'shepherd and sheep' is of course problematic in many ways in a modern and postmodern climate. Not only does it ring with paternalistic overtones, but it is also demeaning of persons on the receiving end of leadership and care-giving ministries. Henri Nouwen is the pastoral and contemplative theologian who wrote most illuminatively on the theology of the 'wounded healer'. Several attempts have also been made (for example, the musicals *Jesus Christ Superstar* and *Godspell*) to present musical portrayals of Jesus as a comedian whose wise folly transformed history.

A problem with all imagistic approaches though is that images lose their appeal or else become unfamiliar and thus lose their ability to communicate. Such has been the fate of the image of shepherd in modern and postmodern urban settings. The quest for newer and more easily understood images runs the risk of producing unconvincing results that appeal only to a few and that soon become obsolete.

Another important approach to Scripture has been described as 'informative'. This is based upon a number of crucial insights into the nature of the Bible as text, and of pastoral care. Premised upon the recognition that both Bible and pastoral care are highly diverse, varied and complex in nature, there is the recognition that there can clearly be no simple relationship between these two areas of study and practice. Since such is the nature both of the biblical text and the practice of pastoral care, there is a real need to explore the different genres and forms of the literature and of the interpretive strategies adopted in relation to the Bible. Similarly, the varying forms and practices of pastoral care need careful examination in any attempt to relate them to Scripture in beneficial ways for the praxis of pastoral care. Donald Capps's book, *Biblical Approaches to Pastoral Counseling* (1981), illustrates this pastoral approach with Scripture. Capps vividly and penetratingly explores how the book of Proverbs may be related to educative pre-marital counselling; how the genre of 'parables', especially in the Gospels, may illuminate marital counselling and how the psalms of lament may critically inform bereavement and grief counselling.

A fifth way in which study of Scripture has been related to pastoral care is through the discernment of deep structures within biblical literature. This is a process in which underlying themes and unifying conceptual threads are discovered through a close study of Scripture. These themes are then examined for their pastoral implications. William Oglesby's *Biblical Themes for Pastoral Care* (1980) is an illustration of this method. Oglesby, as others have, identified four grand themes in Scripture – namely, God, humankind, sin and salvation. He then proceeded to draw out five sub-themes with pertinence for pastoral care – 'initiative and freedom', 'fear and faith', 'conformity and rebellion', 'death and rebirth', 'risk and redemption'. Engagement with texts wherein these themes are apparent, in dialogue with the situations and practices of pastoral care, results in pastoral theology that is valuable to both biblical students and pastoral care-givers.

What is of value in these modernist approaches to Scripture, in the exploration of pastoral theology, is that they take Scripture as necessary and relevant to the pastoral task.

They also make a careful study of Scripture imperative and incumbent upon the pastoral theologian. Moreover, they see a vital connection between practice and text. Although most pastoral theologians recognize the connection, they differ as to the extent to which Scripture or experience is privileged in pastoral theology.

The rise of pluralism and postmodernism has coincided with literary critical and deconstructive approaches to Scripture and their appropriation in pastoral praxis. Whereas in the modernist approaches described the emphasis tends to be upon the text, a greater emphasis on readers, both historic and contemporary, and their response, is evident in the more postmodern or pluralistic approaches to which we now turn. These approaches look primarily and more closely at the audience or presumed recipients of scriptural writings and what their responses were likely to be. They also consider contemporary readers and their responses to texts. Important studies of this shift that has 'allowed for incredible diversity in models of interpretation as well as for thoroughgoing reformulation of the role of culture and experience in the task of (biblical) criticism' (Segovia, 2000, p. 3), have been undertaken, among others, by the likes of Fernando Segovia in the USA and R. S. Sugirtharajah (1991/1995, 1998, 1999, 2001, 2002, 2003) in Britain. Among these pluralist pastoral engagements with the Bible are the hermeneutical, narrative, liberative, feminist, womanist and postcolonial approaches.

Hermeneutical readings follow what has been called the 'hermeneutical circle' in which any reader comes to the text with pre-understandings and pre-conceptions; the text provokes, shocks, vexes or resonates with the reader; the reader dialogues with the text and also other readers and then returns to re-engage the text. This entails a cyclical process in which there is a constant dialogue between readers, backgrounds and social locations, and texts. The socio-cultural, socio-economic, psychological and political contexts of texts, target audiences and contemporary readers are brought into dynamic interaction in this engagement with Scripture.

Narrative readings focus on the power of story and seek an interaction between the story in the text and the stories of the readers. African American Professor Ed Wimberly illustrates this well in *Using Scripture in Pastoral Counseling* (1994). In this book Wimberly draws on narrative biblical criticism and the psychology of narrative to suggest a model for pastoral counselling using Scripture and case studies to explore and release human possibilities.

Liberative readings generally follow a trajectory of approaching the Bible from the perspective of the poor, the marginalized or the oppressed. Suppressed voices in the text, as well as readers in analogical positions, become the hermeneutical key for understanding and appropriating texts. R. S. Sugirtharajah's award-winning volume, *Voices from the Margin* (1991/1995), is a sterling exemplar of the liberative approach. Itumeleng Mosala's *Biblical Hermeneutics and Black Theology in South Africa* (1989) is another worthwhile example of this approach. Mosala explores, among other things, the book of Micah and the first two chapters of the Gospel of Luke, employing both a materialist critique and the historical and cultural struggles of Black people in apartheid South Africa in the development of a Black pastoral theology.

African American womanist biblical scholar Renita Weems, in pursuance of more liberative readings, carefully identifies oppressive discourses recorded in the Bible, especially in relation to the normalizing of violence against women by the way in which women's bodies have been used, assumed and destroyed in portions of Scripture (Weems, 1995). Weems makes reference, for example, to Jephthah's daughter in Judges 11, sacrificed because of a vow Jephthah made to God in payment for victory in battle; the virgin daughter of Gibeah and the Levite's concubine in Judges 19, raped and then dismembered, and Tamar in 2 Samuel 13, raped by her own brother. She writes: 'the correlation drawn repeatedly in prophetic literature between divine judgment and husbands battering their wives is haunting and telling' (p. 3). Feminist biblical criticism enables us to see connections between patriarchy and violence against women. Moreover, African woman biblical scholar Musa Dube, in a pioneering work, *Postcolonial Feminist Interpretation of the Bible* (2000), demonstrates the significance of both postcolonial theory and feminism in biblical studies. Dube's work draws our attention to the interconnections between patriarchy and imperialism and urges the reading of 'sacred and secular texts, ancient and contemporary texts, and imperializing and decolonizing texts, side by side' (p. 199) to highlight, among other things, 'that in the postcolonial era literary practitioners can be categorized into decolonizing, collaborating, or imperializing communities of reader-writers' (p. 200).

Asian American biblical scholar Gale Yee has been in the forefront of an important approach to Scripture known as ideological criticism. This approach studies the values and interests that are embedded in texts. Yee discusses both an 'extrinsic' and an 'intrinsic' ideological criticism of texts (Yee, 1995, p. 147). Extrinsic analyses examine the social and historical environments in which a text was produced, while intrinsic analyses focus on the content (what the text actually says) and the rhetoric (how it is said) of the text. A valuable example of this is contained in *Women, Ideology and Violence* (2004), written by African American biblical scholar Cheryl Anderson. In this book Anderson critically studies gender construction and especially the treatment of women in the Book of the Covenant (Exod. 20.23—23.19) and the Deuteronomic Law (2 Kings 22—23). In the face of unspeakable violence against women historically and contemporaneously, such study of foundational texts is pastorally imperative.

These pluralist approaches have offered both method and content to what can be termed pastoral encounters with the formative texts of Christian traditions. Their pastoral significance lies in the fact that they take very seriously the experience and context of both text and readers. They are theological because they address issues of faith and the interrelationships between God and humankind. They illuminate the ways in which texts and Scriptures influence our formation as people of faith and as such our practices of care, by sensitizing us to particular issues and normalizing other issues for us. In these and other ways practitioners of care engage and are engaged by the Scripture. Scripture continues to influence our reflective practice of care.

Experience

A major source for pastoral theology has been pastoral 'encounters'. Essentially any interaction between a pastoral care-giver and another person in which there is consciously or unconsciously an exchange that can be explored in terms of care, is understood as a pastoral encounter. The Clinical Pastoral Education (CPE) movement has documented and almost sacralized these encounters through the device of the *verbatim*, a written account of verbal and other exchanges usually between a pastoral care-giver and a hospitalized patient. These are then presented within a peer group and discussed with input from a trained supervisor.

Following a clinical practice model, pastoral theologians have utilized case studies as another fertile source of experiential material for theological reflection. Here ongoing encounters between care-givers and clients are recorded, suitably disguised to respect confidentiality, and discussed in one-to-one or group supervision sessions. In this way pastoral theology has been generated in close contact with real life experience. Charles Gerkin demonstrates a 'narrative, hermeneutical methodology for doing practical theology' (1997, p. 18), drawing on experience with individuals in *Living Human Document* (1984), with congregations in *Widening the Horizons* (1986) and within the wider community in *Prophetic Pastoral Practice* (1991).

Pastoral theologians consistently insist upon the crucial nature of concrete human experience in the generation of pastoral theology. Thus, programmes of training, as well as academic courses in pastoral theology, have generally included as of necessity an experiential component.

Context

Several important epistemological shifts occurred within the twentieth century. One of them was the realization of how context and social location influence all knowledge. In theology this understanding is both old and new. In one sense it is a departure from traditional understandings of theology as an objective science declaring universal truths. In another it is a rediscovery of the particularity of the incarnation. Jesus was a Palestinian Jew who grew up in Nazareth. Each of the Gospels and Epistles was written with a specific audience in view. This fact influenced what was said and how it was said. Context, to a very large extent, shapes and informs practice. Context and social location are very evident even in the most abstruse philosophical discussion. As human beings, we are culturally and historically bound, and are socially and psychologically conditioned to interpret reality in accordance with these limitations. Even when we think and act counter-culturally we do so in terms of the cultures we react against and with the tools (for example, language) provided by the culture. In those terms it is interesting to observe how words and structures of language mirror and shape perceptions. Classic examples of this are Eskimo peoples, who have many different words for 'snow', or Filipinos, who have particular names for different forms of rice, enabling them to reflect what persons, whose words for these items are less nuanced, may never fully appreciate.

The stream of consciousness which has been described as *postmodern* includes a recognition and reappraisal of subjectivity and context. As Jencks puts it, 'Postmodernism means the end of a single world view and by extension, "a war on totality", a resistance to single explanations, a respect for difference and a celebration of the regional, local and particular' (1992, p. 11). Theologians now increasingly affirm the importance of 'mediated meanings'. 'Reality', says Bevans, 'is not just "out there"; reality is "mediated by meaning", a meaning that we give it in the context of our culture or historical period, interpreted from our own particular horizon and in our own particular thought forms' (2002, p. 4). Bevans is right when he writes:

> Not until our own time (as we have reaped the positive benefits of the Enlightenment's discovery of subjectivity and the nineteenth century's discovery of historical consciousness) have theologians been so aware of the importance of context in constructing human thought and – at least in the minds of some – of the sacredness of context in terms of God's revelation. (p. 5)

The very nature of pastoral theology urges attention to context. The experiences, world view and perspectives of persons domiciled within poor, urban ghettoes within the slums of a city in the Two-Thirds World will significantly differ from those of persons living in the affluence of suburban western villas. Careful contextual analysis, whether it is of social, cultural, economic or political circumstances, enables pastoral theological work to be more in touch with real life experience and thus to be more relevant and 'true'. Contextual analysis forms the core of the second chapter of this book.

Human sciences

The pastoral theological task, which essentially is one of care for the totality of human experience, is a *multidisciplinary* one. It requires the analytical skills of different disciplines as context determines. As such, pastoral theologians tend to develop the skill of *interdisciplinary* dialogue and practice. This entails an attitude and orientation of respect, humility and collaboration towards other disciplines that also seek an understanding of and care for human persons and societies. Traditionally, pastoral counselling has been developed in dialogue with the disciplines of psychology, particularly psychotherapy, and medical and health care, especially psychiatry. Pastoral counsellors are trained to integrate the disciplines of theology and psychology in their therapeutic endeavours. It is important to realize that the psychotherapeutic disciplines have also more recently drawn on the pastoral theological disciplines in response to their concern to provide a 'spiritually and religiously friendly' practice. A recent example of this can be found in the book *Encountering the Sacred in Psychotherapy: How to Talk to People about their Spiritual Lives* (2002), written by James L. Griffith (Professor of Psychiatry and Neurology at the George Washington University Medical Center) and Melissa Elliot Griffith (a licensed psychotherapist and marriage and family therapist).

Pastoral care has begun more explicitly to draw on a broader range of disciplines, including sociology, anthropology and cultural studies.[4] The dialogue partners have included disciplines of community studies, social ethics and, more recently, economics.[5] The challenge for pastoral theologians lies in recognizing distinct differences between the assumptions and presuppositions upon which different disciplines are based, respecting these while seeking a coherent and constructive dialogue between them. Pastoral counsellors recognize that in the earlier years of the development of their practice, psychology seemed to supersede theology. The desire in response has not been to jettison the human science of psychology but rather to inject a more appropriate balance into the relationship and thus to facilitate a healthy respect for the differences and the potential collaboration between theologians and psychologists. A critical and creative poise is what is sought in the dialogue and interaction between practitioners of different disciplines in the care of persons. Pastoral theologians must make their contribution on the basis of and from the perspectives of their primary activity as theologians.

Summary and questions for further consideration

1 Pastoral theology is defined as *reflection* on the caring activity of God and human communities. How do you understand the four features of pastoral theological reflection mentioned in this chapter? Are they sufficient?

2   Pastoral theological work is undertaken by all who engage in various forms of caring practices related to faith. Is this too wide in scope? Why?

3   Pastoral theology is understood as a form of practical theology. It is an example of *practical divinity* that attempts to hold theory and practice together in dialectical tension. It is thus described as a 'praxeological' discipline. How does praxis differ from practice? How useful is this distinction?

4   Pastoral theology examines both practices of care that are inspired by faith and the forms of faith that are encouraged by caring practice. Reflect on these two dimensions and explain them further. Can an adequate faith be built on the basis of reflection on caring practice?

5   Pastoral theologians approach Scripture in a variety of ways. Review the ones mentioned here. How do you approach the Bible? How does Scripture inform your practices of care?

6   How important is experience in pastoral theology? Think of concrete examples and explore how you would move from experience to theology.

7   All knowledge is mediated through meanings shaped by context. How is knowledge of God shaped by context?

8   Pastoral theology is multidisciplinary. Which disciplines would you consider crucial and why?

9   What is necessary for interdisciplinary dialogue? How can such dialogue be facilitated?

2

Pastoral Theology as
Contextual Theology

Pastoral theologies by their very nature arise out of particular contexts. Social, economic and cultural context to a large extent influences what is available, relevant and necessary for pastoral theology. Contextual analysis can be understood as a way of discerning and seeking to hear what God may be saying out of the different exigencies of the human condition as experienced in different contexts. It is also a means of understanding the reality of the human experience that pastoral theologians seek to care for. Careful attention to historical, socio-economic, cultural and political circumstances is crucial for theological discernment. In a world currently characterized not only by modernism but also by postmodern and postcolonial criticism, this aspect of pastoral theology has great significance. Subjugated and marginalized peoples are increasingly being recognized as sources of authentic and crucial knowledge. It is time for us all to listen to and learn from 'the least of these' (economically speaking), whose traditions most often are both ancient and rich with wisdom for living.

American theologian Edward Farley insists, as we have highlighted, that theology involves, as of essence, 'interpretive-thinking' acts (Farley, 2003, p. 7). Significantly, interpretation, he writes, 'always and inevitably begins with and reflects the historical time, culture, corruption, language, and bias of its own situation' (Farley, 2003, p. 7). Hence it is of utmost importance that pastoral theologians pay attention to the contexts in which they work and interpret the experiences of those they work with, as well as their own, in context.

Contextual analysis includes an examination of social, cultural, economic, political and religious factors at work in given geographic locations. Identifying these factors is one thing. Recognizing their individual and collective impact is another. Moreover, because each of these is never static, a thoroughgoing contextual analysis is necessarily dynamic and historical, exploring changes through time. Further, because these factors do not act in isolation, ways in which they have interacted up until and including the present time, need attention.

In this chapter I will illustrate contextual analysis in pastoral theology by reference to changes in the practices of pastoral care and counselling in different parts of the world, making reference to what has been called the 'Two-Thirds World', in line with the contention, made earlier (see pp. 28–30), that the scope of pastoral theology in the twenty-first century has to be global.

Contextual issues in evidence globally[6]

Wherever one is located in the world today, it is possible to analyse and interpret pastoral care and counselling through the lenses of *three* types of processes. I describe these as *globalization*, *internationalization* and *indigenization*. Although each of these historical processes could be identified and described by itself, there is mutual influence among them in any given local situation.

Globalization happens when, in whole or in part, the lifestyle, world view, values, theology, anthropology, paradigms and forms of practice developed in North America and Western Europe are exported or imported into different cultures and contexts. The term 'globalization' has been used in many different ways and is, of course, itself ambiguous. Nevertheless, there are some realities that appear to underlie all usages of it. Joseph Stiglitz, winner of the Nobel Prize in Economics in 2001, describes globalization as:

> the closer integration of the countries and peoples of the world which has been brought about by the enormous reduction of costs of transportation and communication, and the breaking down of artificial barriers to the flows of goods, services, capital, knowledge and people across borders. (Stiglitz, 2002, p. 9)

What is clear is that the flow, in terms of products, lifestyle and values, has overwhelmingly been from the economically advantaged towards the less well off. Although there are some notable exceptions in socio-economic terms (for example, Japan) this has most often meant from the West to the rest. Nevertheless, subjugated knowledges and cultural practices continue to have marginal impact in the West in the form of 'alternative' lifestyles and religious activities. In economic terms it has been the rich and powerful nations and international institutions that have written and enforced the rules that have to be followed by all people everywhere. These regulations and practices have clearly served the economic benefit of the affluent. Globalization in pastoral care and counselling has followed similar social and economic patterns. Likewise, for centuries forms of Christian faith have been transported from these same western centres into different parts of the world in what can be termed theological globalization. As such, paradigms of pastoral theology evident in non-western contexts often bear the hallmarks of western thinking and influence.

In studying and analysing any context in the world today, whether it is in the North, South, East or West, the effects of globalization come into play. Such has been the global impact and influence of western world views, politics, economics and lifestyles that it would be impossible to understand contextual issues anywhere without an understanding of processes of globalization.

Globalization occurs wherever the practices encouraged and in which local people are trained are the dominant approaches and models of the USA and Western Europe. In the 1970s when I was a theological student in Ghana, West Africa, our main textbook for pastoral counselling was Howard Clinebell's *Basic Types of Pastoral Counseling* (1966). I later learned from a colleague who comes from the Island of Fiji that this same book was their text there as well. A Finnish student of mine in Britain in the 1990s had used the same text to gain a basic understanding of pastoral counselling in the 1980s in her school in Finland. Our practice of pastoral counselling in Africa, the Pacific and Northern Europe was shaped and influenced by one North American author's insights. The content of that text made little or no reference to context. It assumed that all persons everywhere shared the assumptions and presuppositions inherent in middle-class North American society. A study of contextual practices of pastoral theology anywhere has to reckon on the influence of the West.

The mentality of many local people is such that they believe implicitly that things imported from the 'First World' are *ipso facto* superior to what is locally produced. This social, cultural and economic climate is conducive to globalization. In the face of economic, social and political upheavals in many African and Middle-Eastern countries, there are many who call for 're-colonization by the West' or else more rapid westerniza-tion in the guise of technological advancement. Globalization is an inexorable fact of international relations at present and has been beneficial in some respects to all concerned. Never-theless, a great deal of ambivalence exists in non-western con-texts about the processes of globalization that all realize are at work, especially regarding culture and identity. Contextual analysis anywhere has to attempt to trace the historical and contemporary influence of processes of globalization.

By *internationalization*, I refer to processes in which an attempt is made at dialogical engagement, where western understandings interact with non-western ones in a quest for pastoral practices that fit more closely with the cultural and social norms and mores of specific contexts. Internationalization is premised upon an increasing recognition and valuing of 'difference' between cultures and contexts, together with respect and interaction between cultures, nations and social groups. In this process there is an attempt to place western theories and practices alongside non-western, local ones in order to facilitate the development of creative and/or integrative approaches relevant to the local contexts. The International Council on Pastoral Care and Counselling (ICPCC), formally established in 1979, has sought to encourage such dialogue. The Society for Intercultural Pastoral Care and Counselling (SIPCC), inaugurated in Germany in 1995, works along similar lines.

Contextual analysts must figure out the nature of the interactions that are taking place between local understandings and powerful foreign ones in the practices in evidence in local situations. This is true of creative productions in many places. On several occasions while I was working in England, I had the experience of taking newly arrived graduate students from India to the local 'Balti' restaurants in Birmingham. I usually invited them out with a sense of pride that multicultural Britain could give them a tasty meal from 'home'. Without exception the meals were enjoyed, though they each made it clear that there were no *Balti* (meaning 'bucket') restaurants at home and that the meals had clearly been prepared with a European palate in mind. In all local situations it is necessary to explore the creative ways in which persons are seeking to blend their cultural heritage with the realities of dominant cultures and influences. This potent reality forms an important part of most contexts.

Indigenization occurs when models and practices indigenous to non-western contexts are re-evaluated, re-adopted and utilized in pastoral practice. In line with postcolonial cultural, social, linguistic and political criticism, indigenous practitioners of healing are increasingly being encouraged to have an impact within the halls of power in the practice of pastoral care and counselling in several places in the world.

This is happening at various levels within countries as well as between them. Indigenous pastoral theology emerges when practices geared towards healing and care nascent within local contexts are explored. Contextual analysis entails an unearthing of the curative rites and rituals of local peoples.

Contextual analysis in pastoral theology, then, involves the search for an understanding of the world views and practices by which a people care for themselves. This search needs to recognize the ubiquitous presence of the West. It needs also to be sensitive to creative ways in which people blend the influences that they receive. Moreover, contextual analysts need to press forward to touch those beliefs and practices that originate within the culture they work in and which may have been the focus of the inquiries of anthropologists or may have lain silently dormant or else have been virulently suppressed for centuries. Examples of these practices are the works of Eastern shamans and African priest-healers (pejoratively described as 'witchdoctors' or 'fetish priests'). In these practices are embedded a depth of understanding yet to be fully explored, which bears witness to the fact that the God of all creation has not left any people or culture without evidence of the divine presence and the caring love that we are claiming is a focus of pastoral theology.

Historical developments

Historical studies such as those undertaken by Clebsch and Jaekle (1964), John McNeill (1977) and Culbertson and Shippee (1990) point out that the early Church and, before it, philosophers, and even earlier Egyptian sages, sought to heal, sustain, guide and reconcile persons and communities using *iatroi logoi* (healing words). Forms of what we now describe as pastoral care and counselling, which seeks to integrate theological and psychological insights in bringing relief to suffering people, have existed and been practised in very many cultures for millennia.

The earliest roots of pastoral care and counselling, and also of pastoral theology, lie in the healing and restorative rituals and arts practised by priest-healers and sages in antiquity. These ancient traditional healers often combined the roles of priest, therapist and physician. Such persons were the ones to whom people in crisis, danger, or else seeking guidance in life, would resort. The general expectation with which they were consulted was that they would offer words, rites or rituals grounded in culture, world view and belief, which would be effective in bringing relief or else offering meaning, explanation and treatment strategies for traumatized persons and communities. Traditional priest-healers, as such, were knowledgable concerning a wide range of physical, emotional, spiritual, social, cultural and psychological phenomena. Sages made use of traditional insights into life available in sayings, proverbs, stories as well as texts and art works to help people find meaning in, or else relief from, the various maladies they experienced. To the extent that they attempted to make sense of the experiences of the people who consulted them and to critically, interpretively and constructively give expression to restorative care drawing on divine sources, these traditional priest-healers and shamans were the pastoral theologians of yesteryear. They continue to play a similar role in rural African and Asian settings.

One of the features of pastoral care-giving in different historic times has been a dependence upon the cultures, reigning philosophies and psychologies of the periods in which it has been practised, a point made very clearly in the historical work of Clebsch and Jaekle (1964). In that sense, the forms of pastoral care and counselling that have been practised in western societies in the twentieth century reflect the dominant social, cultural, theological and psychological theories of the West. As such, one needs to realize that there are real differences between theories and practices of effective pastoral care and counselling in different parts of the globe, reflecting the very real contextual differences that exist.

A study of developments in pastoral care and counselling throughout the world very quickly picks up broad differences between western and non-western thought and practice. Wicks and Estadt (1993) edited a volume in which the experiences of pastoral counsellors, trained in the United States, at work in ten different countries, namely Australia, Ghana, Kenya, Korea, Malawi, The Netherlands, Panama, Thailand, Venezuela and Zambia, are recorded. In all cases these practitioners had found it necessary to modify the western-based training they had received with its assumptions and presuppositions in order to practise effectively in their culturally distinct contexts.

In what follows, painting inevitably with broad brush strokes, I shall attempt to characterize dominant trends in pastoral care and counselling in different regions of the world. The importance of contextual analysis lies in the ability to locate practice within its historical, geographical and theological context.

The exercise of exploring pastoral or other practice within a context other than one's own may prove helpful in clarifying the contextual nature of one's own practice and could enable one to perceive other ways of caring that could be fruitful even in one's own backyard. Augsburger makes the point that a person who only knows one culture actually knows no culture:

> In coming to know a second or a third culture, one discovers how much that was taken to be reality is actually an interpretation of realities that are seen in part and known in part; one begins to understand that many things assumed to be universal are local, thought to be absolute are relative, seen as simple are complex; one finds that culture shapes what we perceive; how we perceive it and which perceptions will be retained and utilized. (1986, p. 18)

Augsburger realizes that 'knowing another culture may free one from or freeze one to the culture of origin' (p. 18). Like him, it is my hope that this exploration will do the former. Namely that, rather than lead to cultural 'encapsulation' and confirm views of superiority, the exposure will forge creative thinking and new patterns of pastoral theology out of contrasting perspectives. People of all backgrounds may benefit from the contextual analysis that exposes them to different perspectives, enabling them to understand the values that are at work within them.

Western pastoral theology

When compared to practices in non-western contexts, the forms of pastoral counselling which have been developed in the United States are, by and large, individualistic, rationalistic, emotional-expressive, with a focus on the promotion, development and fulfilment of the self (ego) above all else (Halmos, 1965; Lambourne, 1974; Holifield, 1983; Wilson, 1988). This is in line with a system of thought that is essentially materialistic and consumerist, and which, as a result, places the greatest value on acquisition and self-enhancement. As Colin Lago and Joyce Thompson have argued (Lago and Thompson, 1996), western forms of knowledge tend to be external, the result of counting and measuring, with the 'knowers' distancing themselves from the objects to be known. Pastoral theology developed in the West basically follows this pattern, although there is a fair bit of theological critique of these dominant cultural patterns.[7] In point of fact the critique makes clear the very nature of the context against which many critical pastoral theologians protest.

Lest the West be conceived of in monolithic terms it is important within this broad description to distinguish various strands and emphases. For one who has spent a vast amount of my professional life in Britain and being now for the last few years domiciled in the United States, the differences within and between nations that are perceived from outside as constituting 'the West' are very apparent. Pastoral theology in Britain to a much larger extent follows paradigms of 'social justice' and 'education for cultural enrichment', while in the United States it is my perception that pastoral theology is very much closer to the therapeutic and medical models. To recognize these differences one need only compare some of the writings from major pastoral theologians from these two countries. In an essay in *The Blackwell Reader in Pastoral and Practical Theology*, entitled 'The Emergence of Pastoral and Practical Theology in Britain', Paul Ballard (2000) points to the highly secularized nature of British society, with fewer people going to church and less money to spend on historical resources. He highlights the turn to the human in theology, to the practical in education, to the laity in pastoral care and the continued promotion of social action as hallmarks in the development of British pastoral theology in the twentieth century. Growing diversity characterizes developments at the end of that century and the beginning of the twenty-first, with British pastoral theologians welcoming and enjoying the 'breadth, width and inclusiveness' (p. 67) of practical theology in Britain today.

John Patton's 'Introduction to Modern Pastoral Theology in the United States' precedes Paul Ballard's essay in the *Blackwell Reader*. Patton points to the tradition of philosopher-psychologist William James, congregational minister, hospital chaplain and founder of Clinical Pastoral Education, Anton Boisen, and academic professor Seward Hiltner, as shaping modern developments in pastoral theology in the United States. It is clear from Patton's work that Clinical Pastoral Education – with its focus on experience in hospital or clinical settings – has been the major source for the development of US pastoral theology. Along with this has gone certification, accreditation and licensure for practice as mental health practitioners within a system of managed care, absent from the British context. Thus in the US environment, clinical expertise measured through certification has dominated the discussion and development of pastoral theologians.

British pastoral theologian Stephen Pattison's *A Critique of Pastoral Care* (1988/1993) was published in fairly close juxtaposition with Charles Gerkin's *The Living Human Document* (1984). Whereas Pattison challenges too close an identification of pastoral care with counselling, Gerkin's work focuses on the counselling relationship and uses Ego Psychology and Object Relations Theory in the development of a hermeneutics of the self and the life of the soul.

Secularism in the USA manifests itself in a totally different way from the British version. While US churches are still well attended and civil religion thrives in public discourse, British theologians seek ways of engaging in their art in public. A book I contributed to while teaching at the University of Birmingham in the UK is entitled *Dare We Speak of God in Public?* (Young, 1995). This book is a wide-ranging discussion concerning the problems and joys of speaking theologically in education, the academy, therapeutic counselling, in the public square, in global politics, after the Holocaust and in prayer. It is not a title that I have been inclined to recommend or put on a reading list in the south east of the United States! This also highlights the challenges I have faced in trying to write a book that would be valuable in both Britain and the United States, knowing full well that the very nature of the discussions in these two contexts of the West alone would be different and at points mutually exclusive.

However, the core values of western pastoral theology have proved influential in very many parts of the world, not least in areas where totalitarianism and communitarianism have held sway. Chinese as well as Korean pastoral theologians have commented on the value of the focus on individual, intra-psychic and psychological processes within their local contexts where for centuries community and social concerns have subjugated the individual almost to extinction.[8] In such places, personalism that emphasizes the importance of the individual is an important antidote to the oppression of persons through totalitarianism that rides roughshod over individual rights. Moreoever, externalism, with its emphasis on and quest for 'objective' knowledge free from the contaminations of emotion or personal preference, has proved important in the development of science. Much of our knowledge and understanding of the physical world and the environment has come about through the methods developed by western science.

Bearing in mind the pluriformity of the 'West' I wish to mention briefly a kind of reverse globalization that is manifest not merely by the presence of persons whose historical origins lie outside Europe but also by the diversity that was unleashed upon Europe when the Berlin Wall was breached in 1989.

The widening European context

The Society for Intercultural Pastoral Care and Counselling (SIPCC), based in Düsseldorf, Germany, represents a highly significant development in the practice of pastoral care on the global scene. Since the late 1970s, Helmut Weiss, German parish minister and CPE supervisor, has been in the forefront of this movement for internationalization in pastoral care and counselling. Beginning in 1986, when Helmut Weiss invited US pastoral theologian Howard Clinebell to stimulate international dialogue at a gathering of German practitioners on the theme 'Hope and wholeness in a threatened world', 'Intercultural Seminars' were held in Kaiserswerth, Germany. The aim was to enable German practitioners to develop and hone their practices through exposure to and encounter with practitioners from different cultures. These gatherings have projected a veritable trajectory in which there have been encounters between Western and Eastern Europeans in the face of the rapid socio-economic change initiated with the collapse of the Berlin Wall in 1989. These encounters of the 'new expanded Europe' have been a very important source of intercultural learning.

The SIPCC invites practitioners and teachers in the fields of pastoral care, counselling, therapy or other disciplines from all Christian denominations or other religions desiring to improve their helping skills to learn in an intercultural setting. In this approach,

Participants *encounter* people from other cultures and

exchange various cultural experiences. They give and receive new impulses for new *lifestyles*. They give and receive new impulses for their *spiritual and communal living*. They reflect on cultural, social, political, economical and religious *contexts of people*. They challenge their own cultural and religious *assumptions and presuppositions*. They present their *practices in care and counselling* and reflect upon them from various perspectives. They extend their *professional knowledge* in dealing with the theme of the seminar. They enter into a process of *theory building* of Intercultural Pastoral Care and Counselling. (From the website www. sipcc.org, February 2003, emphasis in the original)

The emphasis is upon face-to-face encounter and exchange with people of different cultures and latterly also religious traditions. There is an overt and clear ethos of learning to overcome racist, sexist and other dehumanizing attitudes and behaviours. Moreover SIPCC 'encourages exchange between and meeting humans of other cultures as neighbours and the creation of community with them in an open and fearless atmosphere' (www.sipcc.org, February 2003). There is an express aim of reducing violence, imperialistic imposition and cultural indifference. This process is described as 'intercultural', and bears the hallmarks of the international model explained in this chapter.

From West German beginnings, SIPCC now has an international executive committee and between 80 and 120 participants at its annual gatherings, including significant numbers from Poland, the Czech Republic, Switzerland, The Netherlands, France, Estonia, Romania, Hungary and Great Britain. Each year there are also participants from Africa, Asia and Latin America, most often as speakers and workshop leaders who enhance intercultural encounter, exchange and learning. The SIPCC can genuinely be described as a European movement that has had a significant impact upon the development of models of practice and theory of pastoral care and counselling that takes human diversity seriously within an internationalist framework.

One of the most fascinating encounters I recall was at a conference under the aegis of SIPCC held in Gross Dölln at a former Stasz (East German secret police) camp converted into a church educational centre. It was one of the first face-to-face encounters between pastoral practitioners from the East (Germany, Poland, Czech Republic) and the West. The perceptions and communications were reminiscent for me of some of the conversations between West Africans and their European former colonizers in the late 1950s and early 1960s.

In the new Europe, distinctions between West and former East continue to collapse as new relationships that subsume rather than transcend the past are forged.

Pastoral theology in the Asia-Pacific region

Asian conceptual systems in particular are characterized by a tendency to emphasize cosmic unity and place much value on the cohesiveness of groups. In Asian contexts both inner and external ways of knowing are important, and the aim of knowledge, learning and healing practices is the integration of body, mind and spirit, which are considered to be different aspects of the same oneness (Lago and Thompson, 1996, p. 86). Most Asian contexts are religiously plural, with Christianity historically being a relatively late addition. Asian cultures and religions espouse rich and ancient heritages of healing, care and guidance.

By specific reference to three Asian cultural contexts (Filipino, Chinese and Indian) I will attempt to articulate and illustrate aspects of pastoral theology within the Asian context. In line with the critical, constructive and interpretive activity which pastoral theology is, I shall be reviewing and interpreting the state of the theory and practice of pastoral care and counselling within this region.

Methodist Bishop of Singapore and medical doctor, Revd Dr Robert Solomon, in a keynote address at the 2001 Asia-Pacific Congress on Pastoral Care and Counselling, highlighted seven contextual concerns for pastoral care and counselling in Asia.

They were as follows: globalization, the growth of technology, explosion of knowledge, the new economy, violence, poverty and HIV/AIDS. In order to respond in helpful ways to these contextual realities in the face of rapid and relentless social change, Bishop Solomon urged Asian-Pacific pastoral practitioners to 'take serious consideration of the part played by socio-cultural forces in shaping the values and personalities of people'. 'Counseling', he continued, 'cannot be confined to the counseling room in Asia or be organized simply along a clinical professional approach. Helping people cannot be relegated to the privatized sphere. It must be a personal act in a public world' (Solomon, 2002, p. 111). In line with Asian cultural anthropology, Solomon places pastoral care and counselling squarely in the communal arena. The care of the individual in this model needs to go hand in hand with the care of the community. 'We have to modify hitherto dominant models in counseling, rediscover some old but helpful ways of understanding the pastoral care of communities, and see that pastoral care and counseling has to have both prophetic and therapeutic functions in community' (pp. 111–12).

Solomon argues that in the Asia-Pacific region, tradition and modernization exist side by side and in a mutually influential relationship. As an illustration Solomon mentions the Iban, an indigenous people of East Malaysia, who traditionally live in communal long houses where their lives and economies are organized in terms of this form of communal living. As a result of rapid urbanization, young Iban people are moving to towns and cities where they suffer disorientation and other forms of psychological and social distress. As a pastoral response attempts are being made by the Church to build communal housing for these Iban in the cities in order to minimize the disruption of their social and cultural lives in the new urban environment. Significantly also, Iban Christian leadership is re-examining Iban traditional rituals and customs to recover pastoral aspects of these so that the community can be helped to cope with modern pressures. Indigenization is taking place as these traditional people try to draw on their ancient heritage and customs to find ways of dealing with modern and even postmodern realities.

Bishop Solomon's thoughts about a future shape of pastoral care and counselling in Asia are illuminating:

> For the future we may have to rethink our approaches in pastoral care and counseling. The community itself may need to be seen as the client or patient. Theory-building activities must take place and we will have to help communities in the way we have been helping individuals and families. We may have to think of how communities experience stress, anxiety, grief, loss, identity crisis and depression, and of how they develop, and suffer dysfunction. We will have to study the secret of resilient communities, communal myths, scripts, coping styles and so on. We will also have to deal with issues of justice and compassion for these are important markers of the health and well being of a community. (p. 113)

Solomon's paradigm of seeing whole communities as the clients of pastoral care and counselling embraces a Christian theology of the cross as adumbrated in Ephesians 2.14–16, where the enmity between Jews and Gentiles is resolved by the discovery of a transcending corporate identity and reality in Christ. 'This spirituality of finding larger transcending identities that can bring healing by bringing people together in peace is central to a pastoral care approach to communities that are divided and estranged from other communities' (Solomon, 2002, p. 115). Solomon's pastoral theology is also very contextual and demonstrates a careful analysis of socio-economic and cultural realities prevalent in the region. Asian emphasis on the communal within a context of religious pluralism raises important questions for pastoral therapeutic practice in general and for pastoral theology in Asia specifically.

Asian case study 1: The Philippines

The Philippines is mentioned as the first South East Asian country in which US styles of pastoral counselling took root. Clinical Pastoral Education began in the Philippines in 1964. The Clinical Pastoral Care Association of the Philippines (CPCAP) was started in 1965 (Dumalagan et al., 1983). Numerous denominations from the Roman Catholic majority through mainline and evangelical churches have been involved in this enterprise. An Asian Clinical Pastoral Education Association offers CPE training in Metro Manila and Baguio, as does St Luke's Hospital. These centres attract students from many other Asian countries, thus having a significant effect on the shape of the practice of pastoral care and counselling throughout Asia. This is a prime example of globalization. The global, however, does not represent the whole picture. Fred Gingrich's research (2002) points to several distinguishing features of counselling in the Filipino context.

- Because Filipino culture tends to be less time-bound, directive and linear, counselling in that context may not always fit into the fifty-minute slot.
- Counselling in this context needs to be more flexible, relational and concrete.
- Clients prefer to see counsellors they know personally rather than complete strangers.
- In view of the high value placed on family decision-making, family honour and authority, counsellors need to give special attention to the role of authority figures and family support.
- The belief in the influences of the unseen world of spirits and powers is strong and needs to be taken seriously in pastoral counselling. An important instance of this is the fact that pastoral counselling in the Philippines inevitably faces the issue of *sinapian* (possession or oppression) by the demonic. In Filipino life there is little problem with the interface between the psychological and the spiritual. Pastoral counsellors need to articulate theologies that will assist them in engaging in contextually appropriate responses to this phenomenon.
- *Hiya* (shame, embarrassment, losing face, having a sense of propriety) is a pervasive cultural dynamic that is one of the determinants of valued social behaviour. Pastoral counsellors have often to help clients 'save face'.

- In the face of colonial denigration, economic deprivation and social pressure there is a widespread sense of pain, anger, powerlessness and helplessness, which make up the psychological framework within which much pastoral counselling is done. Gingrich writes: 'Sikolohiyang Pilipino (Filipino psychology) represents the desire to develop a Filipino identity and consciousness apart from colonial heritage' (Gingrich, 2002, p. 16).

An important reference point is the work of Filipino psychologist Enriquez especially articulated in a book entitled *Indigenous Psychology and National Consciousness* (1994) which, as a result of extensive linguistic and field survey methods, rejects the continuation of a colonial mentality among Filipinos and the imposition of oppressive foreign psychologies upon local people. In place of these culturally and psychologically destructive impositions, Enriquez develops a Filipino psychology based on what he describes as a core Filipino value, namely *kapwa* (shared identity), which is related to the interpersonal value of *pakiramdan* (shared inner perception). Evidence of indigenization has already been presented in a book edited as far back as the 1970s, by Mercado (1977), entitled *Filipino Religious Psychology*, which describes medico-religious therapy and counselling in popular Roman Catholic practices and in indigenous churches and sects.

In the Philippines, then, globalization and indigenization are processes that coexist. To understand and develop Filipino pastoral theology we need the contextual analysis of both Dumalagan (Filipino) and Gingrich (US). Both help us see how the global and the local are operating in a specific context in the quest to care for persons.

Asian case study 2: Chinese cultural contexts

In Chinese traditional thought the self cannot attain wholeness except through integration with others and the surrounding context. Thus, following the writings and teachings of Confucius (551–497 BC), *Jen*, translated as benevolence, perfect virtue, goodness and love (Lee, 2002, p. 123) is the basis of all goodness. Etymologically the Chinese characters for *jen* comprise the word for 'man' and the word for 'two' (community). Persons, then, find their identity – and the ethical basis for their lives – in society. 'A virtuous man is one who lives in harmony with others' (Lee, p. 123). As a result of this way of thinking, it is evident that pastoral counselling that emphasizes collective harmonious relationships and family wellbeing is better suited to Chinese persons than overly individualistic approaches.

According to Confucian teaching regarding psychological health, composure, satisfaction, calmness and poise are crucial. As such, for the traditional Chinese the sign of maturity is the ability to appear calm, cool and collected – containing rather than expressing one's emotions. Such Chinese 'reserve' is not to be interpreted as an absence of feeling. Rather, it is the expression of ideals and values that are highly cherished.

Another important Chinese concept with implications for pastoral care and pastoral theology is that of *Li*, which means 'rules of propriety, ritual and good form'. Making reference to the classic Chinese text, *The Works of Mencius* (Book III, Part I, Chapter VIII) Lee asserts:

> *Li* is the code of propriety in the five dyadic relationships: Between father and son, there should be affection; between ruler and minister, there should be righteousness; between husband and wife, there should be attention to their separate functions; between old and young, there should be proper order; and between friends, there should be faithfulness. (Lee, p. 124)

The term 'methodological relationalism' has been used to describe the reciprocity, interdependence, inter-relatedness and good order that is envisaged within Chinese traditional communal life. Challenges in families and society arise where male positional power in what is a largely patriarchal social structure is misused, leading to chauvinism and spousal abuse, among other forms of oppression.

Simon Yiu Chuen Lee's (2002) work has focused on pastoral care and counselling within Chinese culture, focusing on Hong Kong and Chinese immigrants in Canada. As among other Asians, the pervasive influence of traditional Chinese cultural ways upon the lifestyle, personalities and practices of Chinese people is recognizable in these communities.

Family therapy is recommended especially because of the pivotal place of the family as a unit. Simon Lee finds that the work of Berg and Jaya (1993) with Chinese-Americans offers useful insights for family therapy among Chinese people everywhere. Factors emphasized in this work include:

1   Problem-solving techniques need to emphasize negotiation rather than confrontation, with the therapist acting as an authoritative mediator.
2   Clients need to be seen separately before family members are seen together in family sessions.
3   Due respect needs to be given to the head of family.
4   The vertical, hierarchical structure of the Chinese family differs from the more horizontal, 'democratic' style of most North American and Western European families.
5   Family members should never be embarrassed in front of each other.
6   Family relational approaches often prove more useful.

Internationalization appears as the main process through which pastoral care-givers in Chinese contexts are seeking to offer their ministry. Sensitivity to the cultural background of particular Chinese communities in terms of historical and geographical location appears to be the key to pastoral care and counselling among these communities. Internationalization here involves critical dialogue between East and West. The concept of 'differentiation' in family therapy plays an important part in this dialogue. Differentiation has to do with individuals being able to distinguish themselves from the family 'mass' without emotionally cutting themselves off from the others. The delicate balance of self identification and the recognition of thoughts and feelings that do not originate from self within a family setting in a context in which family togetherness is highly valued becomes a therapeutic and theological aim. Discernment is also needed to determine the extent to which specific people, generations and communities have been affected by traditional and non-traditional ideas regarding issues of relationships, individualism, power, authority and societal roles. Traditional Chinese values and norms are taken seriously. Choices are made for family therapeutic models of care as most fruitful in the dialogue with western approaches.

Asian case study 3: Indigenization in India

Indigenization in the Asian context is perhaps most marked in India where ancient Hindu and Yogic rites of meditation and therapy continue to enjoy widespread interest and practice. An example of this can be found in the *Swami Vivekananda Yoga Anusandhana Samsthana*, a global movement active in over twenty-four countries, with headquarters in Bangalore, India. This association aims at bringing the benefits of yoga to the whole of Indian society and indeed the whole world. Through scientific research the Centre seeks to demonstrate and prove medically the health benefits that may accrue from meditation. The abode of peace (*Prashanti Kutiram*) is the name of a spacious campus, the headquarters of the association, where health care and training in meditation are on offer. Here also scientific research is conducted into the effects of the practice of yoga by highly qualified medical and scientific personnel trained in western medical sciences. Recent studies have included investigations into metabolic changes during yoga practices and the effect of yoga on the personality development of students. The Pastoral Care and Counselling Association of India (PCCAI), revived and renamed at a national conference held in Bangalore in July 2001, recognizes work that has been done before in the dialogue between Hindu philosophy and Christian faith. Among other things, PCCAI is exploring ways in which this rich heritage might be drawn upon to provide philosophical, theological and therapeutic models for a more relevant and effective practice of pastoral care and counselling in India and beyond. What is being attempted is a constructive attempt to take seriously an incarnational theology that demonstrates respect for all people, as created in the image of God and therefore requiring to be taken seriously with all their beliefs and practices.

In order to take context seriously within Asia, especially India, it is necessary to seek an understanding of different religions and to dialogue creatively with practitioners of Hinduism, Buddhism, Jainism and Islam, among others. This is done best where all religious practitioners work together for a goal that benefits the human community. Health care provides that focus here. Pastoral theology that emanates from this context can offer tremendous insights for other plural contexts such as exist in the West.

Pastoral theology in African contexts

African systems of thought and practice are based on a spiritual ontology and pragmatic philosophy that places greatest value on relationality. Knowledge is acquired through intuition and the revelation that comes through participation in ritual, symbol, ceremony and rhythm. The focus of healing and counselling is upon the relationship existing between persons and among groups whose intrinsic worth is to be found in the network of spiritual, familial and inter-generational bonds within which they are embedded. Religion and views of transcendence are pervasive and resilient in all of African life. There is little or no separation between a 'sacred' and a 'secular' realm. All life is both sacred and secular. These beliefs are expressed most clearly in rituals that are meant to foster and enhance harmonious relations between humans and the unseen world of ancestors, gods and spirits. Ceremonies, rites and rituals emphasize the importance of participation, symbolic representation and celebration.

Traditional African life and thought provide the framework and backdrop against which the practices of pastoral care and counselling across the continent may be appropriately understood. Centuries of interaction with European and North American philosophies and understandings have resulted in modification but not vitiation of the traditional African mindset. It is possible to speak of an African cultural milieu that is manifest in assumptions and practices. This milieu is observable within diasporan African communities such as can be found in the Caribbean, South and North America and Europe. Among the most obvious of these assumptions and practices are the following:

- Religion has a pervasive and enduring place in life. So embedded is religion in life that many African languages do not have a specific word for 'religion'. Religion is not a distinct compartment. Instead, it is a discernible strand in the tapestry of life. The 'sacred' and the 'secular' cohere strongly without contradiction or confusion. Life at all points is both sacred and secular.

- The cosmos is inhabited and animated by numerous unseen forces, spirits and gods, among which are the ancestral spirits – human spirits of departed members of the living human community. These forces have a crucial relationship with the physical and material forces of humanity and society. People may acquire knowledge and skill in interacting with the unseen forces. Such skill may be used for good or ill.
- For human wellbeing and flourishing there has to be harmony throughout the cosmos. The ancestors as intermediaries between the seen and unseen forces of creation are arbiters of this harmony.
- A holistic and synthetic view of life prevails. The different aspects of human, social and spiritual life are connected and interpenetrate.
- There is a communal view of life that emphasizes a sense of belonging, rather than an individualistic one that values aloneness.

An African Association for Pastoral Studies and Counselling (AAPSC) was formed in 1985 following an ecumenical consultation on African pastoral studies organized largely at the initiative of Congolese pastoral theologian Dr Masamba ma Mpolo. The African Association's objectives include promoting pastoral studies and counselling from a 'distinctly African' perspective, and fostering awareness of the 'spiritual, psychological and social processes taking place in Africa as they relate to pastoral studies and counselling' (Masamba ma Mpolo and Nwachuku, 1991, p. 5). It is significant to note that the spiritual is primary in the processes considered important for pastoral studies and counselling in Africa. This is in keeping with the world view sketched above, where spiritual forces are seen as crucial in life and therefore in any form of pastoral practice.

Two books published under the auspices of the African Association capture the emphasis of African pastoral care and counselling. These are *Pastoral Care and Counselling in Africa Today* (1991) and *The Church and Healing: Echoes from Africa* (1994). An earlier work edited by Masamba and Kalu (*Risks of Growth: Counselling and Pastoral Theology in the African Context,* 1985) contains relevant insights into the nature of pastoral dynamics in various parts of Africa. In these works, responses to globalization are offered, though internationalization and indigenization are very much the preferred processes. Masamba offers an integrative vision bespeaking internationalization, in which pastoral practitioners, 'work towards the integration of the cultural, psychological and theological disciplines, helping us to explore the insights of these disciplines in relation to the ministry of the Church in today's Africa' (Masamba ma Mpolo and Nwachuku, 1991, p. 27). He nevertheless remains convinced that pastoral theologians in Africa 'have to take into account the African dynamic interpretations of illness and health' (p. 27) in diagnosis as well as in treatment strategies giving voice to indigenous sentiments. Masamba's work thus revolves around beliefs and practices that have occupied a central place in much African discourse, especially to do with illness, misfortune, anxiety and mental ill-health – namely, 'witchcraft' in Africa. His approach seeks to be quintessentially African:

> Disease in Africa is thought of as also having spiritual and relational causes. It may be ascribed to bewitchment, to the anger of mistreated and offended spirits, to possession by an alien spirit, or to broken human relations, pastoral counseling should therefore also use spiritual means of letting people deal with their emotional needs, even through ecstasy, rituals and symbolic representations. (p. 28)

Two books written by Ghanaian pastoral theologian Abraham Berinyuu, *Pastoral Care to the Sick in Africa* (1988) and *Towards Theory and Practice of Pastoral Counselling in Africa* (1989), also helpfully explain contextual pastoral issues faced by pastoral theologians in Africa. In the latter, for example, Berinyuu presents divination as an African form of therapy, because it is a model that seeks to efficaciously respond to the question on the minds of traditional Africans when confronted with any form of suffering or misfortune, namely 'Why?' The African diviner not only diagnoses but also offers effective remedies for the condition (Berinyuu, 1989, pp. 38–49). This work highlights and questions significantly the theological underpinnings of African pastoral practice, thus illustrating the need for pastoral practitioners to engage in both religio-cultural and theological reflection upon the data, beliefs and practices nascent within their context.

What seems significant about all researchers and writers on African pastoral care and counselling is that they engage with indigenous people's beliefs and the practices of traditional healers in their attempt to evolve a truly African approach to pastoral care that is relevant and effective. Berinyuu's 'divination' and Kasonga's 'African Christian Palaver' (in Lartey et al., 1994, pp. 49–65) are illustrative of this. The overriding model is that of indigenization. However, there is, in almost all cases, also a desire to engage with western theory and understandings in an international, dialogical approach, often reflecting the framework of training or education that most African pastoral theologians have had. To this end it can be argued that African approaches to pastoral care, counselling and pastoral theology are largely indigenous and international.

Pastoral theological developments in Latin America

An exploration of pastoral care and counselling in Latin America is best approached from two arenas – Protestant and Catholic. Protestant or Evangelical pastoral care has largely followed the process of globalization. James Farris, from the USA, who is Professor of Practical Theology at the Methodist

University of São Paulo, Brazil, points out the lack of organizations in Latin America for pastoral counsellors and outlines the extent of dependence on US and European sources by reference to the texts used in seminaries and universities, almost all of which are translations from Spanish-speaking countries, the USA or Europe (Farris, 2002, p. 245).

It is in Catholic or what is known as *Pastoral Popular* (Popular Pastoral Care) that one hears the voice of the *pueblo* (people) – especially the poor – in Latin America. What is common to both Protestant and Catholic forms though, reflecting the reality of the context, is that 'there are no private practice models for Pastoral Counseling' (Farris, 2002, p. 245).

Sara Baltodano, Professor of Pastoral Care and Counselling at the Universidad Bíblica Latinoamericana in Costa Rica, helpfully draws on translations, indigenous publications, as well as booklets and pamphlets by Latin American organizations, to illustrate the nature of the practice of pastoral care and counselling in the region. While Protestant approaches to pastoral care in Latin America have tended to follow the globalization route, Catholic approaches have been more closely tied to Latin American liberation theology. To that extent Catholic approaches have been more indigenous in method and ethos. With the exception of a growing interest in systemic approaches to pastoral care in some organizations, Protestant pastoral care in Latin America has followed the largely individualistic approach of US Protestant models. Baltodano points to ecumenical and Evangelical bodies such as CEDI (Centro Ecuménico de Documentacão e Informacão) in Brazil, CELEP (Centro Evangélico Latinoamericano de Estudios Pastorales), a continental organization with its headquarters in Costa Rica, and CEDEPCA (Centro de Estudios Pastorales en Centro America) located in Guatemala, which aim to broaden the concept of pastoral care and counselling to include collective action by the Church (Baltodano, 2002, p. 204).

Influenced by *Gaudium et Spes*, the famous papal encyclical issued by the Second Vatican Council that studied the role and function of the Church in the modern world, a new Roman Catholic approach to pastoral care in Latin America, based on liberation theology, has emerged. This form is defined by its focus on the care of the Latin American poor, who are, in fact, the majority of the population (hence it being called 'popular'). Although not necessarily the form adopted by Catholics across the continent, Popular Pastoral Care is increasingly well developed, especially in Brazil and Nicaragua.

Brazilian Protestant philosopher, theologian and psychoanalyst, Rubem Alves, arguably the first to articulate a theology of liberation, has been in the forefront of the ecumenical dialogue around liberation theology in Latin America and beyond. Alves argues persuasively that 'pastoral care is determined by its institutional setting' (Alves, 1977, p. 127). 'Pastoral care', Alves declares, 'is located institutionally. It can only exist within a specific social organization that has certain problems to be solved' (Alves, 1977, p. 127). Hence,

> If pastoral care is socially determined by the functional relationship between, on the one hand, individual-congregational needs and, on the other, its ability to respond to these needs, the ultimate criterion for its success is whether it contributes to the unity, well-being, and growth of the congregation. (p. 130)

Popular Pastoral Care, recognizing the social, economic and political environment within which it is embedded, seeks to respond appropriately. As Baltodano says, 'Pastoral Care means both transforming the immediate situation of a family who must watch the death by hunger of their child and the transformation of society such that this tragedy no longer happens to any child: a new creation' (Baltodano, 2002, p. 205).

A cardinal principle of Popular Pastoral Care is that the poor are agents of their own liberation, not merely subjects of the pity and action of others. Following Clodovis and Leonardo Boff, Baltodano presents the concept of the existence of only 'one history', in which God is acting through the poor such that the poor are active subjects who participate in the process of their own liberation and are not merely passive objects. As such, Popular Pastoral Care travels with the poor as they seek their liberation. Rejecting hierarchical, top-down approaches to pastoral care, Latin American theologians and people have embraced Basic Christian Communities (BCCs) as the locus through which care is mediated. These small groups (of approximately ten people), meeting in houses, chapels or under trees, are made up of ordinary people – domestic servants, peasants occupying land without title or owner-ship, bricklayers, industrial and agricultural workers, rural migrants to the city – all believers, not all 'poor or oppressed', gather together to reflect on their faith and act caringly within their communities. In terms of pastoral care BCCs try to fulfil two aspects, namely to take care of individuals, families and small groups, and to serve as agents of social change in the community. These coincide with the pastoral aims of Popular Pastoral Care – personal care and care of communities.

The method of working within the BCCs begins with living together, building trust and confidence and breaking down class barriers. The next step is to restore the voice of the poor through listening and encouraging them to speak for them-selves and tell their own story. It is important also to relate people's stories to the history of the nations or the world, giv-ing context and significance to the people's story. The over-arching aim of all these acts of 'seeing, judging and acting' is to work creatively for a truly gospel-oriented and directed revolution. 'Such a revolution involves all realms: politics, economics, family, culture, and religion. In other words, everything related to society' (Baltodano, 2002, p. 212).

Pursuing these aims, Baltodano proposes a *liberating pastoral care* of the poor that encapsulates the theological insights of liberation theology together with a deep knowledge of the situation of the poor in Latin America. Such an approach takes into account the culture of the poor and recognizes the poor as active subjects who are able to change their own situation. Liberating pastoral care is a hope-filled vision and struggle with the complex problems faced by poor families in Latin America. Thus emerge forms of pastoral care, counselling and pastoral theology that are indigenous, communal, socio-economically informed and relevant to the context.

Rationale for contextual study

By means of these all-too-brief aerial snapshots of different regional contexts I have sought to illustrate what is involved in contextual analysis in pastoral theology. David Tracy urges all practical theologians to pay attention to both local and global situations. He writes:

> Some dialectic of the local and the global . . . presses upon all practical theology worthy of the name. To assume that only the 'local situation' or only the 'global situation' demands attention is to down-play, however unconsciously, the full demands of all practical-theological analyses of the 'situation'. (Tracy, 1987, p. 140)

I concur entirely and offer the following four distinct reasons why in this work I have sought to engage different geographical and cultural contexts and why I think contextual study is crucial for all pastoral theology.

First, this chapter has sought to encourage all pastoral theologians to undertake an analysis of their own contexts with the realization that personal needs that call for pastoral responses in each context are embedded in the social, economic, cultural, religious and political issues unearthed and explored thereby. Second, we have sought here to draw attention to the fact that historic processes, such as globalization, have succeeded in transmitting particular values throughout the world. Although responses differ from place to place it is possible to discern similar trends in different locations. It can be useful for westerners (and non-westerners as well) to explore how what was constructed in their context historically has influenced practices in different parts of the world. Third, this study of developments in pastoral care in different regions has served to introduce us all to different realities being faced by people in different contexts and to take a look at the responses being developed. Taking context seriously means realizing that people really are different and face different issues. Finally, this chapter has sought to foster a sense of solidarity in the midst of difference among all pastoral theologians. Pastoral theologians are summoned by the God *of all creation* to the task of caring. As human beings, no human experience is totally foreign to any one of us. We can all learn from attention to human experiences, no matter how different the cultural or economic circumstances within which they are enshrined may be. In theological terms, the ultimate context to be analysed by all pastoral theologians is the *global context*, not simply and exclusively their own little corner. However, the best way to do this is to listen deeply, and with empathy and interpathy,[9] to the experiences of 'others' from distinctly different contexts, without seeking to subsume them into our own. A healthy respect for the otherness of others is a contextual and core value and discipline of pastoral theology. Pastoral theology is contextual theology precisely because it engages in the analysis of local and global contexts as an intrinsic part of its practice.

In Chapter 4 (see pp. 93–120), where we examine more closely the 'content' of pastoral theology, we draw on these contextual analyses in articulating the understandings of the nature of God and of faith that are embedded in the practices of pastoral care explored here.

Summary and questions for further consideration

1   Contextual analysis aims at understanding the reality of human experience, recognizing that experience is shaped, coloured and influenced by context. Offer and discuss some examples of this.

2   Contextual analysis opens up a way of discerning what God may be saying through and to humanity. Consider some examples of theological insights gained through attention to context.

3   Globalization, internationalization and indigenization appear to be all around us. How do you understand these processes? What response do you make?

4   Contextual analysts have to trace historical influences. They must also explore the interactions taking place between local and foreign understandings in every place. Examine some examples.

5   Contextual analysis involves a search for an understanding of the world views and practices by which people seek to care for themselves. Consider some examples.

6   Pastoral theologians are urged to be both local and global in their contextual perspective-taking. How might this be possible?

7   The earliest roots of pastoral theology lie in the interpretive, healing and restorative rituals and arts practised by priest-healers and sages in antiquity. What and how can we learn from these?

8   Western models of pastoral care and counselling tend to emphasize the individual and reason (insight), and promote selfhood. Explore strengths and weaknesses of this emphasis.

9   Asian conceptual systems tend to emphasize cosmic unity, communitarianism and group cohesion. Examine strengths and weaknesses in this.

10   The major focus of healing and care in African systems of practice is upon the relationship existing between persons and among groups. The worth and dignity of persons is found in the network of spiritual, familial and interpersonal bonds within which they are embedded. Examine strengths and weaknesses with this.

11   'Popular' Pastoral Care in South American contexts has developed mostly in response to people's experience of poverty. What can be learnt from this context about caring?

12   The poor are agents of their own liberation, not merely subjects of the pity and action of others. How can this insight be operationalized in pastoral care? What are the characteristics of a *liberating* pastoral care?

3

Methods of Pastoral Theology

Kathy (35) is considering whether to arrange for her mother (Sarah) to be placed in a home for the elderly. Her fiercely independent mother expresses the view that she can manage very well on her own. She has nevertheless been found on a number of occasions wandering around her neighbourhood at unusual times. Kathy feels guilt-ridden and accused as not caring for her mother, but also does not feel she should impose her views on Sarah. She feels torn between a realistic assessment of her own ability to care for her ageing and ailing mother, Sarah's own very strong and clear views about not wanting to be abandoned to 'rot' (her words) in an old people's home, and her feelings of obligation to one who gave up much of life's comforts to ensure she had a decent life.

Joe (30) feels under pressure from family and friends to 'settle down' in life through establishing a long-term marital relationship. He is ambivalent and is thinking through his options. He has good male and female friends. He remains in a state of uncertainty about his own sexuality and is not prepared to make a 'fool of himself or someone else' (his words). He feels quite at ease just as he is, but also feels social pressure either to marry or else to 'come out' as gay.

Both Kathy and Joe have opted to work with pastoral care-givers to explore what they ought to do as Christians. The work they have embarked on will engage them in making pastoral theological judgements and taking actions informed by their faith as well as the realities of their life situation. Pastoral theologians need processes, procedures or simply ways by which they might arrive at, and enable those they work with to make, informed choices about courses of action they might undertake. Pastoral theologians choose among a number of methods, each of which seeks to be truly theological.

Methods have to do with procedures and processes by which desired ends are arrived at. Ted Jennings begins his entry on 'Pastoral theological methodology' in the *Dictionary of Pastoral Care and Counseling* (1990, pp. 862–4) with the following definition: 'The critical evaluation of the procedures for arriving at theological judgments, proposals, or assertions' (p. 862). To this I would add 'practices'. Pastoral theological methods entail procedures for choosing between different theological assertions *and* practices to engage in with integrity and faith. They enable pastoral theologians to determine what practices of pastoral care may be consistent with their faith and most helpful for the persons concerned. They aim at facilitating the practice of appropriate, relevant and consistent pastoral care.

Let us turn now to an evaluation of some key procedures by which pastoral theological judgements are made and how choices of particular pastoral actions are arrived at. The basic question is '*How* do we engage in pastoral theology?' What methods have been and are being employed presently in the formulation of pastoral theological judgements and practices? To be theological in the pastoral sense, following our understanding of the discipline, the methods adopted need to facilitate critical, interpretive, constructive and expressive reflection on the caring activities of God and human communities.

Methods and methodology

Before we proceed, a number of distinctions and clarifications need to be made. Pastoral theological methods are many and varied. The terms 'method' and 'methodology' are understood and used in different ways. Methods are employed for different purposes. Methods of research in pastoral theology, methods of presentation of studies, methods of procedure in pastoral care and methods of theological reflection are examples of different 'pastoral theological methods'. Lying behind all of these are *methodologies* – or theories of method – which we will hint at, for purposes of clarification.

One way of approaching *methodology* is to view the term as referring to the underlying *theory* or philosophy of the method or procedure being considered. A methodology outlines the rationale for a method. For example, 'applicationism' is the methodology underlying different deductive methods in which practices are deduced from bodies of theory or principle. In some forms of pastoral theology, deductions are made from theological, philosophical or scientific theories. Deduction arrives at practice from theory. Inductive methods, on the other hand, begin from 'experience', action or practice and then by various procedures and means generate understandings from analysing the concrete practices. Induction develops theory from practice. Inductionism as such is methodologically opposite to applicationism in its starting point.

Methodologies map out the framework or theoretical environment surrounding choices and decisions concerning appropriate procedures to arrive at desired ends. They offer the logic for and of the method to be followed. As we increasingly become aware of different forms of logic so do we recognize different methodologies surrounding different methods and practices. Practical theologians point to different forms of logic (for example, aesthetic, deductive, inductive) and recognize their validity for a variety of different pastoral practices. A methodology also expresses the ethical framework or sets of values that envelop and define the approaches to be followed.

Research methods are those procedures adopted to search for, explore or seek understanding of a particular subject under investigation or of interest to a researcher. For example, survey methods involve administering questionnaires or conducting interviews with sections of a population. They yield data that may be analysed quantitatively (that is, using mathematical methods), qualitatively (non-mathematically) or in mixed modes that combine qualitative with quantitative methods. Surveys are important for discovering what is going on in societies and thus in seeking appropriate care for persons. As another example, literary methods entail the study of historic texts of different kinds. Such study often helps gain understanding of a means by which some people seek therapeutic ends, namely through writing. Pastoral theologians adopt a range of different research methods in exploring and examining subjects of interest to them.

Methods of presentation have to do with ways of organizing the fruits of research. These may follow closely the research method adopted. Thus a research study of the experiences of clients in pastoral counselling, for example, might be presented by beginning with the reports of the clients (case material). These reports may then be reflected upon using sociological and psychological categories. This might then be followed by theological reflection. Alternatively, the same material might be presented beginning with psychological-type theories, which are subsequently illustrated by the case material. These different procedures follow different forms of logic and flow. Of significance is the fact that the method of presentation chosen is suggestive of the underlying methodology. The prioritizing of different types of data and procedure is indicative of the ideology or ethos of the researcher.

There are very many procedures that are used in the processes of pastoral counselling or pastoral care. In all forms of pastoral counselling, nevertheless, the establishment of rapport between client and counsellor occupies the attention of the counsellor in the initial phases of the process. Psychodynamic pastoral counselling, for example, typically seeks to create an atmosphere of calmness and receptivity through allowing the client to 'free associate' by talking without the fear of interruption, contradiction or censure in the opening phases of the encounter. Methods of procedure in pastoral counselling, then, reflect methodologies that emphasize acceptance of clients as persons of dignity and value, who need, therefore, to be taken seriously.

Methods of theological reflection in pastoral theology are the differing ways in which pastoral theologians engage theological discourse. An approach that has enjoyed much favour in pastoral theological circles has been David Tracy's revision of Paul Tillich's correlational method. In Tillich's theological method the questions raised by our existence and life are correlated with answers to be found in the symbols of the Christian tradition. Tillich writes:

> In using the method of correlation, systematic theology proceeds in the following way: it makes an analysis of the human situation out of which the existential questions arise, and it demonstrates that the symbols used in the Christian message are answers to these questions. (Tillich, 1951/1988, p. 62)

Tillich argues that 'the Christian message provides the answers to the questions implied in human existence' (p. 64).

Tracy revises this unidirectional question-and-answer ap-proach to include questions arising from the Christian tradi-tion and answers from existence. In this way he sets up a dialogical method of 'mutually critical correlations' in which questions and answers flow in both directions between existence and Christian symbol.[10] 'Theology is the discipline that articulates mutually critical correlations between the meaning and truth of an interpretation of the Christian fact and the meaning and truth of an interpretation of the contemporary situation' (David Tracy, in Browning, 1983, p. 62). 'The correlations', Tracy continues, 'are between both the questions *and* responses of both phenomena, the Christian tradition and the contemporary situation, not simply "questions" from one pole and "responses" from the other' (p. 63).

Pastoral theologians have found Tracy's revised correlational method amenable to their purposes of theological reflection on pastoral encounters. This exercise of critical dialogue between experience and Christian symbols constitutes one example of a method of theological reflection.

Gaining an understanding of the methodology and methods employed by a theologian or any other practitioner of an art is helpful in recognizing how they arrive at their conclusions. The same would be true of clients and other care-receivers. If all we have to work with are their conclusions or fixations, we are left with very little that is helpful in understanding them as persons and how or why they are 'stuck'.

Moreover, it is important, even crucial, that methods employed to arrive at positions and actions be explored to enable us to be creative and change approaches that do not really deliver the desired ends. Theologically, methods are the means by which we critically reflect and thus gain a deeper understanding of the divine mystery and the human–divine connection. Let us now examine some of the key methods of pastoral theological activity.

Pastoral theology as *applied theology*

An enduring legacy of the formulation and description of theology as a discipline within the academy, one of the major tasks that engaged the attention of Friedrich Schleiermacher (1768–1834) is the idea of practical theology as 'applied' theology. This legacy, though arguably unintended, continues to exert influence upon the understanding and reception of the disciplines of practical theology especially within the academy in different parts of the world. Schleiermacher envisaged theological 'science' as a discipline worthy of its place in the university. As a discipline akin to law or medicine, he pictured theology as a tree, with philosophical theology as its roots, historical theology as its trunk and practical theology as 'crown' or fruits. His intention was more to map out the core branches of the discipline than to place them in logical or hierarchical sequence. However, by placing and picturing them in the way in which he did, he appears to have led the belief and practice of practical theology as a derived, technical *application* of principles and theories derived from the 'pure' disciplines of philosophy and history to the business of church leadership and management.

This method of arriving at theological judgements and practices is deductive. It involves 'applying' theoretical principles to particular situations. The strategy is one of exploring chosen principles or theories and figuring out how they might apply to the situation at hand. The principles in these cases are derived from Christian doctrine, the Bible, philosophical theology, historical tradition or the teachings of one's faith. These are then applied to the situation of life under question.

While this method affirms the necessary connection between theory and practice, it can be criticized on several grounds. A first criticism is based on the fact that in actuality and historically, life or experience precedes theory. Theory emerges out of disciplined reflection on observed experience. Theory is the result of, and therefore dependent upon, experience and practice. As such, the applied theology model turns actuality on its head and proceeds from theory to experience. Second, deduction only works when a body of theory (based itself on reflection on experience) becomes so established as to become the basis upon which sound practice is deemed to follow. As a method it is dependent on the applicability of the theories it draws on. What applicationism does, then, is to focus on the results rather than the method by which the theory it depends on was formulated. Third, the applied theology model may fail to recognize that theory is itself based on practice and may treat theory as if it were not itself subject to analysis on grounds of experience. In effect it loses the important insight that the theory from which it draws is itself built up out of observation and interpretation of experience and practice. When this happens, historical or philosophical theology is treated like 'law' or legal requirement and becomes subject to the danger of legalism as opposed to grace in Christian thinking and practice. Fourth, the necessary mutual dialogue and critique that enriches both theory *and*

79

practice is lost. In actual fact, to follow his illustrative image, the leaves from Schleiermacher's tree do fall onto the ground and help fertilize the soil and provide nourishment for the roots and the trunk of the tree. Thus practical theology is not merely an applied technique, it may also be the source of significant nourishment for the art and science of theology.

If Kathy's pastoral counsellor were to choose to adopt an applicationist model in responding to the issues she brings she would be looking for a body of principles or theories to give to Kathy. She might search the Scriptures or some classics of Christian faith to try to find some principles about the care of ageing parents that Kathy could apply to her situation. With Joe she might try to find theological material about sexuality that he might read and apply. In both cases the problem would be with the degree of fit between what might be read and the actual life situation and experience of each of them. The linearity of the approach and lack of interaction between text and life situation might prove to be its downfall.

Pastoral theology as *applied social/human science*

Much effort in pastoral care and especially pastoral counselling has found its source of knowledge for practice in the discipline of psychology. The views one holds concerning human persons, and the constructions one has about how humans become the way we are, shape and influence one's proposals for healing and change. Realizing that many issues of human life are being investigated through rigorous scientific investigation by human and social scientists, pastoral theologians have sought to apply the wisdom of these scientists to their caring actions. This necessary appropriation is not without several difficulties. Stephen Pattison, in an important essay (1986), has helped identify some of these difficulties. There is the issue of the vast array of human sciences and sub-disciplines within each, as well as the exploding knowledge base within each one. How does one choose? Which disciplines are relevant and which aspects are to be included? Even when suitable choices of disciplines appear to have been made, how does one keep up with the continuing changes in these disciplines?

Is eclecticism, in which bits and pieces are chosen and then applied in a 'pick-and-mix' fashion, appropriate? Several pastoral practitioners make the claim that they operate in this fashion when they say 'I use that which works for my folk'. However, Windy Dryden, a British professor of counselling psychology, identifies no fewer than *ten* forms of eclecticism (Pattison, 1986, p. 81). The question of the basis upon which selection is premised remains.

There is the very real danger of pastoral practitioners becoming so fascinated by approaches in the human sciences that they become absorbed into these disciplines as amateur (or at times having attained the necessary qualifications, professional) psychologists, psychotherapists, management scientists or sociologists as the case may be. The danger lies not in becoming qualified but rather in the uncritical adoption of presuppositions and practices without the important. contribution of theological critique. Pastoral theologians run the risk of becoming mediocre social scientists espousing out-dated theories in an eclectic and exclusively pragmatic manner.

For the 'application' of social and human sciences to pastoral theology to be properly undertaken it is crucial that a critical awareness be cultivated. Experts in the chosen disciplines need to be consulted and engaged in respectful dialogue. Such experts need to be invited to comment on the way their sciences are being utilized by practitioners of different disciplines. Pastoral theologians may need to become qualified in at least one other discipline at graduate level to ensure that they have a sufficiently informed approach to the dialogue. Assumptions and presuppositions need careful examination because they at base determine the orientation of the practices espoused in any discipline. Pastoral theologians need nevertheless to remember and maintain the fact that they are basically theologians making contributions out of their primary discipline to the task of the care of human persons. Team work, where experts in different specialities work collaboratively and with mutual respect, remains the ideal to be followed.

Pastoral theology as *critical conversation*

A useful way of relating practice and theory is through the analogy of a conversation between partners who are prepared to take each other seriously. This method has the advantage that it makes use of a familiar and accessible image drawn from everyday life to convey an important and difficult activity.

Different theorists suggest different partners for the conversation of pastoral theology. In general, the three most common are:

- a person's ideas, beliefs, feelings, perceptions and assumptions (experience);
- the beliefs, assumptions and perceptions provided by Christian tradition (faith resources);
- the contemporary situation under examination (cultural resources).

The exercise is dialogical through and through in that it entails an engaged interaction between parties. It is, in fact, a 'trialogue' with three conversation partners interacting. Distinct from the applied-theory methods, this approach seeks an inductive and mutually critical interaction in the manner in which an honest conversation would take place. Each participant is committed to stating and clarifying their own views. They are also committed to exploring the views of the others. Moreover, they are committed to reviewing their positions in the light of the dialogue. Where Christian tradition is perceived as 'fixed and unalterable' this latter becomes difficult. However, there are many who see Christian tradition as inherently open and processive and can demonstrate how down through the years Christian faith has shown itself very amenable to creative re-formulation. Examples of this include the ordination of women and most recently the ordination of a gay bishop in the United States.

Stephen Pattison (2000), Charles Gerkin (1997), Paul Ballard and John Pritchard (1996), Chris Schlauch (1995) and James and Evelyn Whitehead (1995) offer examples of pastoral theology as critical conversation. In choosing the metaphor of conversation above that of correlation, the Whiteheads assert, '*conversation*, with its possibilities for interruption, disagreement, and surprise, seems a more adequate image' (p. 4). Whitehead and Whitehead present us with a model or an image of the elements involved in theological reflection and a method that describes the dynamic movement of reflection. Chris Schlauch (1995) refers to this as 'theologizing' to indicate that it is an active process of living and reflecting that we all engage in. For Schlauch, theologizing is practical conversation in which metaphors and narrative are bridges (1995, pp. 29–44).

Kathy and Joe in this model would be in critical dialogue with the faith traditions and the human sciences that speak to their situation. Kathy could raise questions about her own self-care and the nature of mother–daughter relationships. Joe's sense of his sexuality would be a valid conversational partner with traditions of faith that suggest uniformity in sexual preference as the norm. All partners in the conversations would be permitted to state their positions and raise questions about each other's views.

Pastoral theology as *cycles of reflection and action*

Scottish theologian James Whyte distinguishes the types of questions asked by systematic theologians from those asked by practical theologians in the following way: 'The systematic theologian asks critical questions about the way faith expresses itself in language; the practical theologian asks critical questions about the way faith expresses itself in practice' (James Whyte in Campbell (ed.), 1987, p. 213).

The task of analysing the practices of care for their faith

content is then a crucial aspect of pastoral theology. Utilizing the analogy of the three-way conversation we have referred to above to do this, Whyte reminds us of the need to engage three poles in a dynamic interaction:

> Since the Church's life and action is related not only to its own self-understanding and comprehension of its faith, but also to the changing society in which it functions, practical theology is triadic, concerned with the interrelationships of faith, practice and social reality, and is aware that the lines of force flow in both directions. (Whyte, 1987, p. 213)

This dynamism between faith, practice and social reality has marked several models of pastoral theological reflection. This process has been systematized into cycles which proceed from concrete experience (action) through analysis into pastoral responses. Laurie Green's very accessible book, *Let's Do Theology* (1990), is still perhaps the most useful 'pastoral cycle resource book', to quote the book's subtitle. Green proposes a four-stop cyclical process from experience through exploration, reflection, response and then on to new experience. Green developed this method through parish encounters with working-class Christians in Birmingham, England, later discovering that the method of theological reflection he was working with was very similar to the 'pastoral cycle' developed by liberation theologians from a model originally utilized by Father Joseph Cardijn, a Belgian priest who had been an inspiration to many Catholic workers and students during the 1920s and 1930s in Europe. Cardijn had basically tried to encourage Christians to careful analysis of their situation and experiences by asking them to SEE (observe, pay close attention to), JUDGE (analyse and evaluate) and ACT (take reflective action) on their experiences. Green's cycle, or better spiral, moves continually around from action or encounter in situation, to reflection, and back again. Green argues that we begin doing theology by attempting to become as conscious of the real situation that surrounds us as we possibly can. This is what he means by 'experience'. It is a step in the process in which we make every effort to become as aware and conscious as possible about the situation and the experiences – including feelings and impressions – as we can.

Although Green does not make this as clear, it is important to recognize that experience is a mediated phenomenon. There is no such thing as 'pure' experience – no experience that drops from heaven in unadulterated purity. Everything we become aware of comes to us through our internalized processes of analysis and interpretation. This means that experience is always a construction.

The second step in Green's spiral, which he calls the 'Exploration' stage, is an analysis of the situation employing various disciplines of enquiry. Here we attempt to gain perspectives on the situation from sources other than our own immediate interpretations. Questions are asked about individual agency, structural or social factors and power dynamics. This then leads to a reflective phase in which a concerted and conscious effort is made to see how Christian faith relates to the situation under exploration. The genius at this point is to check the situation against Christian heritage and the heritage against the situation. Green suggests that a host of resources such as Bible study, prayer, worship, the creeds and councils of the Church and theologies of times past, are at the disposal of the group that is exploring their situation. Here the complexity of the method becomes apparent. This is the most bewildering aspect of the spiral. Nevertheless, it is the one in which theological resources are most explicit. The final stage is when the group returns to action within the situation with new insights and impetus derived from the process, asking the question, 'What does God now require of us?'

The value of this, and indeed all, cyclical processes lies in the fact that they offer identifiable steps or stages in what could otherwise be a rather amorphous exercise. The difficulty remains that of being clear as to what each stage really entails and determining where and why one enters the cycle at a particular point.

Pastoral theology as *shared Christian praxis*

One aspect of the cyclical process that bears emphasizing is the corporate nature of the exercise. Pastoral theology acquires its sharpness from the fact that it is 'done' in groups. One practical theologian who makes this abundantly clear is Roman Catholic religious educator Thomas Groome. Groome presents the picture of 'A group of Christians sharing in dialogue their critical reflection on present action in the light of the Christian story and its vision toward the end of lived Christian faith' (Groome, 1981, p. 184). This approach integrates a number of important elements from the previous one. There are clearly five components involved – action, critical reflection, dialogue, story and vision. It focuses on present *action*. In this way it emphasizes practice, making concrete the language of experience. Here pastoral theologians are assumed to be engaged in some form of action or activity upon which they reflect. Groome gives the example of a worship service. However, it could be any activity of care, such as building a shelter, serving food or digging wells. Theology then is a second-order activity assuming a prior action upon which one reflects. It thus gives priority and privilege to action, in line with the plea of liberation theologians. Critical reflection is a means as well as a goal of this method.

Groome speaks of a dialectical hermeneutic between Christian thought and the action-in-situation. Dialogue within a group in which each participant speaks their truth openly, being careful and honest in confronting each other and the action under scrutiny, is the way in which this method operates. Groome speaks of 'the Christian story' by which he seeks to emphasize not monolithic truth but the narrative nature of Christian faith. This is to say that Christian faith is approached through encountering the stories of persons (for example, Abraham, Isaac, Jesus, Paul) who struggled to understand and live their lives in faithfulness and obedience to compelling visions.

Kathy, under this method, would be encouraged to join or

else form a small group of persons of faith involved in taking care of aged parents. The group would seek to provide a supportive environment in which all issues faced by each would be a legitimate concern for dialogue and discussion. Leadership would be provided to enable the edge and focus not to be lost. The group would explore resources, including books for help in determining the most appropriate line of action taking both Sarah's and Kathy's situation into account.

Joe would likewise become a part of a group of persons of faith exploring their sexuality within the framework of their traditions, social customs and values. Space would be provided for honest dialogue and exploration of a range of possibilities. An environment of respect and safety would be sought by all.

Pastoral theology as *practical moral reasoning*

Don Browning has long sought to re-establish links between pastoral care and counselling and Christian social ethics. In doing so he inherits the age-old tradition of theology as *habitus* – practical wisdom for living. However, Browning seeks to avoid a narrow pragmatism as well as a mere technical applicationism. He argues that especially in an age of pluralism pastoral care needs to be guided by philosophically oriented practical moral theology. Browning advances three main reasons why such linkage is necessary. First, that practical moral reasoning helps establish the context of values for any relationships of pastoral care and counselling. Second, that practical moral reasoning helps care-givers gain a clearer idea about what is actually going on in any given encounter or situation. Third, that there is the need to establish for the wider community the necessary public and systemic framework of values that guide the work of pastoral care and counselling.

In terms of theological method, Browning espouses the revised correlational method presented by David Tracy. However, as an exponent of a method of practical moral reasoning

Browning offers five levels or types of practical reason and four steps of practical theological action. The levels or types of practical moral reasoning he espouses are the metaphorical, obligational, tendency-need, contextual-predictive and rule-role. These are understood as forms of practical moral reasoning related to people's development and character. They also serve as analytical tools to understand how people arrive at choices as to how they should act in given circumstances.

The four steps in Browning's practical theological scheme are:

1 Experiencing and defining the problem.
2 Attention, listening and understanding.
3 Critical analysis and comparison.
4 Decision and strategy.

In this way Browning combines a conversational with a cyclical approach to practical theological action-taking. Browning is anxious that practitioners of pastoral care and counselling understand and choose to operate out of clearly articulated frameworks. The wider context or network of values always shapes or at least influences what is done in the realm of pastoral care and counselling. Browning, then, is arguing for a pastoral theological (ethical) framework for the practices of care and counselling. In essence Browning's method has to do with establishing theological frameworks for practice and as such his is an example of a method that entails the development of systemic networks and ethical structures as guides for practice.

In pursuing this approach, Kathy and her pastoral care provider would seek wider ethical frameworks within which to examine Kathy's choices. They would see her choices as set within a society and thus having some significance for that community. Similarly Joe's explorations would be set within the wider social, cultural and global debates about sexuality, marriage and honesty. The actions and strategies arrived at would be respectful of both individual choice and moral responsibility within society.

Pastoral theology as *liberating intercultural praxis*

Increasingly practitioners of care have become aware of the crucial influence of social and cultural factors in all that we engage in. All of our experience is socially constructed and culturally framed. We are in a real sense creatures of culture and creators of experience. As such we must pay close attention to the social and cultural location of all persons. Gender, race, class and culture – all constructed features of our existence – are the lenses through which we live and interpret our reality. Our faith, ethics, norms and preferences are shaped within identifiable cultures and honed within specific societies and communities. This is made more complex by the fact of fluidity and movement between and among different social and cultural contexts. No one of us is isolated from the reality of social change and social interaction between and among the social groups in which we participate. Our pastoral theological methods somehow need to take this reality into serious account.

A method of pastoral practice that seeks to do this is one I have developed for my own practice of pastoral care.[11] In essence this approach privileges situated, contextual experience and the analysis of that experience in its multi-layered and multi-factored reality. The cycle begins with concrete, mediated and constructed experience. Attention is paid to experience or practice as a constructed reality in the first instance. The 'stories of our experience' become the material for our analysis. The second phase is named 'contextual analysis' to emphasize the situatedness and complexity of any experience to be explored. Much care must be given to what is always layered. Every mediated experience is multi-layered and needs to be treated and analysed as such. A distinct part of this, named and separated only for the purposes of attention and recognition, is 'theological analysis'. This concerted and considered attempt to ask faith questions is the point in the cycle where theological resources come most to the fore. The next phase is equally theological in that it seeks to demonstrate the

89

dialectical nature of faith and theology. Here situational questions are directed to faith traditions, and faith traditions are examined at the bar of contemporary reality. If the third phase can be in language and ethos 'in-house' or private, this phase is decidedly public. Faith issues cannot pretend to be unrelated to real life situations. The last phase is reflective practice.

Jim Poling, in his book entitled *The Abuse of Power* (1991), adopts an approach to child sexual abuse and domestic violence that epitomizes this intercultural dynamic. Beginning from the account of Karen, a survivor of child abuse and rape, he proceeds to explore and reflect on the nature of human beings, community and God. This painful and atrocious behaviour of persons is explored psychodynamically, sociologically and culturally in an attempt to get at the theological significance and appropriate pastoral theological responses.

Kathy's choices whether to place Sarah in care or not are set within a culture that makes certain assumptions and places certain expectations upon people within it. These would be very different in other social contexts. The existence of homes for the aged is certainly not universal. It would be instructive for both Kathy and Sarah to explore what in historical, social and cultural terms might be influencing their different views about what is best for them by comparison or contrast with others in a similar situation in a different cultural context. How, for example, would an African or Asian faced with these choices respond? What social support systems would be available?

Joe's explorations also have cultural significance and valence, explorations of which could be instructive. The point of intercultural explorations here would not be for one culture to prescribe for another what best practice would be, but rather for the culture-ladenness of the issues to become more apparent. Specific strategies for action will need also to take into account what is socially appropriate. In these, more can be shared about how one employs culture in response to culture-embedded issues.

At the end of this exploration of methods you may be feeling like I did after my first two children were born. As a graduate of psychology and theology and a practising therapist well schooled in the pros and cons of a plethora of child-rearing theories and practices, I felt paralysed – only too aware of the pitfalls in any approach that I might choose to adopt in raising these two young boys. My suggestion after 24 years of child-raising is this. Study carefully as many methods as you can. Study also very carefully the particular situation (child, client, group) you are faced with. Then make a selection on the basis of what seems to you to have best fit – knowing full well that you may be wrong – and then be prepared to change as the situation develops.

Overall, the aims of pastoral theological methods may be summarized into two as follows:

1   To gain a deeper understanding of the nature of the divine, the human and the relationship between them.
2   The development of more appropriate forms of care for persons-in-context as a result of the reflections on the divine nature.

Both of these are appropriately and deeply theological in their significance. Pastoral care finds its true origins and nature in God. It is God who is the primary pastoral care-giver. Thus the development of appropriate forms of care can be seen to be an essential dynamic of pastoral theology in that it is an attempt to discover, reflect and mediate care that is consistent with the nature of God. Through reflective practice of care we may gain deeper understandings of the nature of God. This praxeological means of theological knowledge that we are arguing has been neglected may be very fruitful in both the exploration of the divine nature and the practice of more appropriate forms of pastoral care.

Questions for further exploration

1 How do you understand the term 'methodology'? How does it differ from 'method'?

2 Examine different types of methods related to pastoral practices.

3 Categorize the methods introduced in this chapter in terms of their methodology.

4 Which method appeals to you most? Why?

5 Think about a situation, person or group you are involved with in a pastoral relationship. Outline how you might use each one of these pastoral theological methods in that situation.

4

A Matter of Theological Content: Care-Inspired Faith

> Theology is a way of organizing our thinking about God.
> (Rainbow Spirit Elders, 1997, p. 15)

Judy, a pastor in the United Methodist Church, sits in her office trying to prepare a sermon for Sunday's service. In walk Tommy (48) and Agnes (44) looking tired and distraught. Although Judy does not know them well, they have been fairly regular attendees at her church over the past year. They have not so far joined the church. Agnes's background is Roman Catholic and Tommy's is Baptist and they have been coming to Judy's church in part out of a 'compromise'. The combination in Judy's church of high liturgy and evangelical preaching meets their quest to be respectful of each other's religious heritage. Tommy is African American and Agnes is Asian American. They have three children, aged 10, 15 and 17. The oldest, Grace, will be leaving for university in the next year.

They sit down and tell Judy that their 15-year-old daughter (Tina) has been hospitalized overnight after an overdose of alcohol and drugs. The physician has called in a psychiatric consultant for Tina, who met her this morning. The psychiatrist suggested, among other things, that the daughter might be depressed and will need continued assessment, and that the family might benefit from family therapy.

Agnes tells Judy that they cannot afford treatment, and that Tommy was fired from his job two months ago and that, moreover, she had always been the primary breadwinner. Tom's recent firing had only exacerbated tensions around his sense of inadequacy. Agnes has been concerned about Tom's increased alcohol use, cessation of normal activities, and his isolation from others. She has found emotional support for herself through a women's group she attends. This group is at the moment almost all white. She is the only Asian or for that matter 'person of colour' who participates in the group. Agnes reports that the family's stress levels have been increasing and that the grades of their youngest child, Sam (10), have been falling. Sam recently fought a classmate at school and bit him on the arm. Tommy's mother who had been a 'tower of strength' (his words) for him died three months ago and he has been 'wondering where God is and whether God really knows or cares about us'.

Agnes, the first of three children, has both parents living, though her relationship with them has been rather cool since her marriage to Tommy. Her father had expressed a view that their relationship was 'unnatural and not in God's design'. Tommy is the third of six children and enjoys a decent relationship with them all, although his involvement with them has been less than deep – they all live in different parts of the country. His father now lives with Tommy's eldest sister.

Agnes becomes tearful saying that she feels scared, angry and confused. She does not know how they will afford university for Grace. Agnes worries about Tommy and what she sees as his growing drink problem since his mother's death. Agnes tells Judy they have come to see her for pastoral counselling and also to ask her to visit Tina in the hospital. Tommy stares at the floor, making no eye contact, with a blank, withdrawn expression. Just as Judy is about to start talking there is a knock on the door. The caller beckons to Judy to come over urgently. There is a message from the hospital: Tina has just died.

Judy returns and enters into conversation with Tommy and Agnes. The first thing she does is to inform them of their daughter's death. The response is devastation and horror. Following a few exchanges in terms of arrangements, they all go out immediately to the hospital.

Over the next six months Judy works with the family offering pastoral counselling and support in their grief and pain. For Agnes the main issues boiled down to her faith and her marriage, which are both 'mixed' (her word). How does God see her? 'This must be God's way of punishing me for marrying a non-Catholic, who is also Black. We met while he was serving in the US army helping liberate my home country from foreign domination. I was convinced our marriage was of God.' Since

the death of his mother Tom had been feeling a sense of alienation from everything that was a source of strength and stay. It
was as if his 'Source of Being' had been snatched away. He often
felt rootless and hopeless. His mother for him had been his connection with the past and with faith. He depended on her prayers
and her confidence. Now everything was coming 'unstuck'. Why
would a God of love take away his source of stay and now also
one source of his hope for the future? He struggled also with the
fact that it was the females in his life that were being taken away.
Would Agnes also leave him?

Theologians have a professional interest in ideas, images,
views, concepts and constructions of God that they encounter
in history, texts, literature, various cultural productions, and in
the stories of people experiencing or perceiving God in different ways. The North American theologian Gordon Kaufman,
for example, argues that the proper task of the theologian is
the continual critical examination and reconstruction of the
symbol 'God' so that it can with greater effectiveness influence
contemporary and future human life (Kaufman, 1978). Other
theologians, with perhaps stronger views of revelation, would
argue that this task is not unaided by a God who wishes to be
known; that our theology is only possible because of the will-
ing self-disclosure and revelation of a God who freely chooses
to be unveiled and known. Consequently the reflections,
articulations, activities and constructions of theologians
enter synergistically into the self-revelation of God. As new
historical, cultural, social and political circumstances have
arisen or been encountered, theologians have re-examined,
reformulated, reinterpreted or reconstructed the symbols of
their faith in response, with a view to presenting the content
of their faith in a way that is relevant and coherent within the
changed circumstances. It is important to recognize that these
formulations are cultural products that are clearly influenced
by a theologian's own psycho-social and political context.

To assert that God wishes to be known and as such may be
present and influential in a theologian's work is a statement
of faith which may serve to inspire prayerful and humble

interaction with God. It may, alternatively, result in arrogance and feelings of superiority on the part of a theologian who may perceive him- or herself as having special and direct knowledge not available to other (lesser) mortals. Every theological construction needs, as such, to be subject to the critique of others within as well as outside the community of faith within which it arises. All theologians need to realize and acknowledge with all due humility that their work essentially remains work in progress and can never be the final or complete word on any subject.

Pastoral theologians are as interested as all other theologians in notions of the being, nature and activities of God. The particular emphasis they bring to the theological task is the exploration of how concepts of God are related to pastoral practice. As a discipline of practical theology, pastoral theology participates in this constructive art by means of *praxis*. As we have seen, in praxis, action and reflection are held together in critical and mutual interaction. As such, pastoral theology is not merely a derived discipline. It does not simply consist in theories, rules and regulations for the practice of pastoral care. Nor is it to be identified solely with the application of theoretical knowledge gleaned from the 'stronger' and more academic disciplines of systematic and historical theology.

Pastoral theology has validity and utility in its own right. It is a *theological* discipline in that it contributes to the study and discussion of the nature of God, humanity and community and the inter-relationships between and among these. Pastoral theology speaks about the nature of God, the nature of human beings and of community, realizing that these three – God, humanity and community – are deeply inter-related. Together these three and the relationships among them constitute the framework and horizon of pastoral theology.

In Merle Jordan's important book *Taking on the Gods* (1986), he presents the work of pastoral counselling as essentially a theological work of engagement with the 'gods' that are at work in the lives of clients. Jordan's pastoral counsellor takes seriously and wrestles with these 'gods', who are often related to the joys and sorrows encountered by the clients. Jordan helpfully distinguishes between 'operational' theology (by which we live) and 'professed' theology (what we say we believe), arguing that it is crucial that pastoral counselling explores much more deeply the theologies (gods) that are in operation in the life of the client and not simply what is professed. A troubled person may profess to believe in a God of love and forgiveness yet live by a God who punishes her at every turn of her life. In fact Jordan is convinced that, often, the problems being faced in counselling occur precisely because of the discontinuity between professed theology and operational theology. The dissonance felt by the client is experienced at the point of this fracture.

Judy explored the constructions of God that seemed to be active in Tommy and Agnes's lives. She was concerned about the punitive God of Agnes. It was important for Agnes to have been able to name her feelings and thoughts. Judy could then explore with her how punishment, which had been a part of her upbringing, could have led to this view. In the face of the tragedy of her daughter's death Agnes could not help thinking that Tina had brought the suffering upon herself and that God, true to form, was there to make her pay for her misdeeds. It was a struggle for Agnes to re-conceptualize God and to dissociate God from the displeased parent with an impulse to make people pay for their wrongdoings.

Tommy's God was a tower – a fortress – of strength to which all people could retreat for nurture and safety. In an intriguing way Tommy's God was also female. The pain he felt, and the alcohol he used to assuage this longing for succour, was deeply connected with feelings of abandonment and the tearing down – as if by military means – of his place of refuge. The juxtaposing of military and domestic imagery for safety and succour was highly significant.

Jordan shows how counsellors' responses may fall into three categories: collusion with the gods; conflict with them; or construction and reconstruction of the gods. Jordan seeks to help pastoral counsellors move from collusion with damaging gods to construction of more appropriate gods. In this regard Jordan's (the pastoral theologian's) practice resembles that of Gordon Kaufman, the systematic theologian, whose work emphasizes the critique and the reconstruction of concepts of God.

Judy sought through pastoral counselling and also by liturgical means to help in the critique and re-construction of the 'gods' that emerged through Agnes's and Tommy's pain. Important therapeutically though was the need for the 'gods' to emerge. Judy had to bear with Tommy and Agnes as they expressed their pain and frustration. She had to appear to collude for images to become clear. Only then could she begin the painstaking work of confronting and re-constructing.

In a similar vein, North American professor of pastoral counselling Wayne Oates (1986) envisioned pastoral counselling as involving exploring the 'epiphanies and theophanies' (p. 32) in which persons describe the presence or absence of God in their lives. Oates sought to reinterpret and reorient the pastoral counselling relationship so that 'the Presence of God [becomes] as its lasting and abiding center' (p. 32). For Oates, pastoral counsellors remind their clients of 'whatever they perceive God to be' (p. 121). Indeed 'their perceptions of God are confirmed, corrected, denied, or reassessed in the process of being in our presence' (p. 121).

Pastoral theologians bring to the theological task encounters, reflections and experiences of human life that help to illuminate, problematize and invigorate theological discourse. Pastoral theology may help us explore more deeply the interrelationships between God, humanity and community. The human–divine relationship, full, as it is, of enigmas, challenges, possibilities and potential is examined with a focus on how caring is mediated within it. Through such examination on the part of pastoral theologians, our knowledge and understanding of both the divine and the human may be enriched.

As we have seen in the previous chapter, pastoral theologians favour a 'praxeological' means of gaining knowledge and understanding of God and the human–divine nexus. Pastoral theology attempts to keep practice and theory in critical dialogue and relationship with each other. Pastoral theologians affirm that we learn about God through practice and action; that significant and substantial knowledge about the nature and activity of God is gained through practice and action.

Pastoral theology is experiential theology – theology through practices and action. God is to be encountered, experienced and understood in part through the art and logic of practice. For the pastoral theologian, reflective practice is a primary means of knowing and understanding God. Indeed, as presented in 1 John 4.7–12, God makes himself known through acts of love and faith. 'Beloved let us love one another, because love is from God; everyone who loves is born of God and knows God' (v. 7). 'No one has ever seen God; if we love one another, God lives in us and his love is perfected in us' (v. 12). It is along the path of love and labour that we find glimpses of the essence and meaning not only of life but also of God.

As pastoral theologians, John and Charles Wesley travelled this path as they sought to spread practical divinity throughout the world in the eighteenth century, blazing a trail that has had worldwide significance. Russell Richey of the Candler School of Theology at Emory University has recently expressed this well:

> The Wesleys . . . and the peoples called Methodist, have imbedded their deepest convictions, their most cherished values, their defining beliefs, and their fondest hopes in practices. On that premise, we argue here that one way to do theology in the Wesleyan spirit is to read practices theologically. (Richey, 2005, p. ix)

However, this is not merely a 'mark of Methodist theology', it is true of all religious practices. All religious practitioners, consciously or not, engage in practices that are value-laden and faith-laden. The craft of pastoral theology entails the reading of practices to discover within them the essence of faith.

British theologian Paul Fiddes, who is of the Baptist tradition, has argued cogently that the doctrine of the Trinity was developed by the early church Fathers not so much out of the study of ancient texts as out of reflection on their experience. The early followers of Jesus had had to rethink their understanding of the being of God as a result of their experience of God's presence and activity among them. Fiddes writes:

> They began with God at work in salvation, healing human life. They had encountered God in the actions and words of a human Son, Jesus Christ; they found God revealed and active in this Son who welcomed outcasts into the Kingdom of God the Father and spoke the word of forgiveness on God's behalf. They found God in a new energy and guidance they experienced within their community, opening up relationships beyond the accepted social boundaries and opening up hope for a future new creation. (Fiddes, 2000, pp. 5–6)

The early Christians chose the revolutionary path of thought that departed from the strict monotheism of their Jewish roots while also challenging the many divine principles of Hellenism. They saw the being of God as reflecting their experience of God as Father, Son and Spirit. Their understanding and presentation of God as Trinity resulted in large part from reflection on their experience and participation in or practice of faith. North American pastoral theologian Chris Schlauch makes the point very clearly when he writes: 'Even the most abstract, formal, systematic, speculative theologizing should be understood as precipitated by and responding to experience and practice in order to enhance future experience and practice' (1995, p. 28).

As such, pastoral theology is not isolationist. It is inextricably linked with other theological disciplines through dialogue and interaction. Much may be learned through respectful listening as historical, doctrinal and biblical theologians engage pastoral theologians in dialogue, in their common quest to explore and express their understandings of the nature and ways of the Godhead. A real contribution of practical theology lies in the efforts it makes at enriching the whole of theology with the insights that emerge from pastoral practice. Where this contribution is properly recognized, valuable theologies are constructed from the margins and fewer theologies are developed that reduce or ignore human experience. Pastoral theology in particular explores all aspects of human experience and resolutely refuses to engage in theological discourse that fails to engage unpleasant or inconvenient aspects of human life. The experiences of victims, survivors and those who have overcome the appalling injustices, indignities and inhumanity inflicted by humans upon fellow humans are included and at points become the central focus of the work of pastoral theologians. Making possible the voicing of the atrocities experienced by survivors of rape, domestic and intimate violence, child abuse, unjust imprisonment, torture and violence is a cardinal aspect of pastoral theology. For confronting these unspeakable horrors brings depth and reality to our reflections on the nature of God, humanity and community.

In this chapter, therefore, an attempt is made to sketch some concrete things that may be learned concerning the nature of God, humanity and community through pastoral praxis. The basic question in this chapter is: what can be learned about the nature of God, faith and theology, through the reflective practice of care? In pursuing this question three important points of explanation are necessary.

First, in the light of an understanding of the world as created by God, we take it that the nature of reality is bound up with the nature of God. That which is real is so because it participates in the life of the Creator. The life and nature of the Godhead is integrally related to that which is real. Although one cannot and must not equate the creation with the Creator, the universe reflects and bears the imprint of its maker. Thus, to speak of God in this way of understanding is to make explicit and implicit statements about the nature of reality. In speaking about God we make implicit and at times explicit statements about the created order and as such what really is. Since God is related to the world in integral ways, nothing that is a part of the reality of the world can be unrelated to God. Theologies are therefore ways of talking about reality in its ultimate and essential form. They examine what is real in the light of reality's relationship with God. The ultimacy of theological discourse lies in its descriptions of reality from particular perspectives. Theology engages in discourse about reality. Theology, thus, has a 'public' aspect and has to engage and be judged on grounds that are open to non-theologians. Theology cannot simply be the esoteric language of an initiated few talking to themselves about a private entity the nature of which is too complex and abstruse for 'common people'. The relationship between the Creator and the created is complex. Nevertheless, all humans to differing degrees engage in reflecting upon the life they live and on the way things are in nature and culture.

Second, in what follows we will be considering the *nature* of the discourse on God, humanity and community; the discourse we refer to as *theology*. One of the ways in which we speak of theology is in the sense of 'rules' or a grammar of faith. In this way of thinking, theology offers us language and grammar (rules establishing the correct use of language) by which we may speak of God and the world. Theology is as much about *how* we speak about God as it is about *what* we say about God. Pastoral theologians are concerned with how we do theology and how we speak of God. We are concerned with the grammar of faith and experience as well as what can actually be said about the nature of God. In other words, we are concerned both with the nature of God *and* the nature of theology. As with other disciplines, the nature of the subject must be related to the nature of the discourse. We must proceed in our conversations about God in a way that reflects the nature of God as far as we have come to recognize God. I contend that among the reasons why theology has at times been unable significantly to inspire and engage the life of people of faith in several places lies in how it has gone about its business. An exclusive focus on abstract, conceptual discourse results in the perception of God as an abstract philosophical concept, having little to do with the really important matters of our lives. This chapter, then, has to do both with the nature of God as well as the kind of theology we engage in. Reference will be made both to the subject of the discourse (namely God, humanity and community) as well as the nature of the theological discourse itself.

Third, pastoral theologians operate within the limitations of human language. While they certainly attempt to be coherent and comprehensive they realize that what they present, in the very nature of things, will only be aspects of the realities they speak about and not the complete picture. Thus pastoral theologians embrace an express hope that what they present will be supplemented by other disciplines. Pastoral theologians 'know only in part and prophesy only in part' (1 Cor. 13.10) and realize that 'we see in a mirror, dimly' (1 Cor. 13.12). Nevertheless, we seek to communicate what we know and see as clearly and coherently as we can in the hope that it will contribute to our collective vision as theologians. In pastoral theology an attempt is made at a forthright statement of what we have come to understand and believe. This is an articulation of faith that seeks to draw from tradition, Scripture, reason and experience, in humility and yet with confidence.

Let us now consider some of the features of theology that pastoral theologians particularly bring to the table out of their pastoral praxis. We shall do so through the presentation of the following ten perspectives.

1 Tentative theology: speaking about a God who can be trusted

A starting point for pastoral theologians is a realization of the tentative nature of all theology. Theology needs to be tentative, reflecting the fact that it represents our feeble efforts to speak about the eternal one who for ever remains 'beyond'.

Given the awesomeness of the theological endeavour a degree of uncertainty is always appropriate. Pastoral theologians encounter the limits of human finitude at all points of our practice. Dealing with devastating and often incurable illness, natural disasters such as the underwater earthquake and tsunami of the closing days of 2004 in which thousands of Asians and others lost their lives, unspeakable cruelty, brutal and senseless violence, emotional and mental distress are the daily round of the pastoral theologian's call.

Contemplating such trauma as evidenced in the global ecological crisis, British theologian Rex Ambler seeks an answer to the question 'Where on earth is God?' The question is particularly framed to reflect the ecological crisis. Nevertheless, the question articulates the cry of persons that pastoral theologians encounter in the different loci where we seek to provide pastoral care. It is a cry of faith as well as distress. Faith and anguish are often close together. Pastoral care providers, like Judy in the case study with which this chapter began, so often encounter people who are asking where God was when particular tragic events occurred. Many live with this question at the centre of their lives.

Ambler suggests three ways of 'locating' God that are all necessary and significant in developing a faith that may orient humankind for the future, namely 'God is beyond', 'God is here' and 'God is ahead'. God is beyond in that 'God is not in any imaginable space in the universe, above or below, but wholly beyond it, unimaginable and unthinkable . . . The experience of God is therefore an experience of the limits of our existence' (Ambler in Young (ed.) 1995, p. 94). Pastoral theologians very often encounter this transcending reality in the face of tragic circumstances. Pastoral theology is articulated and lived at the limits of our human existence.

In another sense, God is here, near and present, in that 'God is not a separate, distant reality but part of the reality of our everyday life . . . But God is not present as an object is present. God is eternal, so God is present to us in another dimension than our familiar dimensions of space and time

(p. 95). Pastoral theologians struggle to articulate and orient us all to this 'other' dimension that impinges on our everyday lives at so many points. The awareness we bring is of the triune One who is closer than a breath and yet further than a cloud. Affirming the presence of God is recognizing a dimension that is other than what is normally referred to and yet is not out of this world in detached disconnectedness.

And yet again, God is ahead: 'God comes to us, not so much out of the past, calling us back to where we were, but out of the future, beckoning us to a new world, that we ourselves must help create' (p. 98). Pastoral theologians recognize and seek to enhance an embracing of that which is yet to be, not in an escapist, ostrich-like, head-in-the-clouds kind of way. This engagement with the future energizes work in the present. It is an engaging to work out the realization of the eschatological hopes and expectations of faith.

Theologians need a suitable humility in the face of their subject. Dogmatism may actually subvert the very nature of theology. Affirmation of faith is important as a point of departure rather than a final destination. God is a reality to be trusted rather than domesticated or 'understood' without remainder. Pastoral theology challenges us all to be people of faith not certainty – to trust in a living and loving Being who is not completely reducible to any system of thought. It is a challenge pastoral theologians face constantly. Lynne Price (1996) chooses the intriguing expression 'Faithful Uncertainty' to encapsulate the theology of British Methodist pastoral theologian Leslie D. Weatherhead (1893–1976), who serves as an early example of pastoral theologians prepared to engage psychology and theology, human experience and divine revelation in mutually critical dialogue. Pastoral presence has to do with being present in such a way that the beyondness, closeness and futurity of God are glimpsed in a uniting, transformative and experiential frame.

2 Provisional knowledge of God

In John 16.12–13 as part of the farewell discourse of Jesus the Christ, we find these significant words: 'I have yet many things to say to you, but you cannot bear them now. When the Spirit of truth comes, he will guide you into all the truth.' Commenting on these words British systematic theologian Gareth Jones writes:

> It is only one verse, but it contains an argument of paramount importance for everything one can say today about Christian self-definition. Jesus Christ is saying that *not everything* has been revealed through incarnation and ascension; *more* will be revealed after Pentecost, after the Holy Spirit has been sent to the Church. . . . The claim here is simple: after incarnation and ascension, more will be revealed *by the Holy Spirit*; revelation continues *in the power of the Holy Spirit*; the Holy Spirit in, by, and through the Church *has its own task*: to lead people further into the truth. The implication here is enormous: the work of revelation continues after incarnation and ascension; the revelation of truth, and consequently, Christian knowledge and understanding of truth is *incomplete*. That the work of the Holy Spirit is genuinely and equally the work of God, and therefore completely identical as willed event with incarnation and ascension – and indeed creation – is vouchsafed by the doctrine of the Trinity. Nevertheless, Christianity lives in and *towards* that power of the Holy Spirit which is in the process of carrying people further into truth. (Jones in Young (ed.) 1995, p. 128)

Pastoral encounters enable us to face squarely the provisionality of our knowledge and articulation. As we gaze into the depths of human suffering, the apparent 'silence' of God and how woefully inadequate our theodicies and theological explanations often are, we come to recognize just how little we know and how few answers we really have. This realization, however, is actually a saving grace because it confirms the inscrutability of the Godhead and the finitude that is the reality of human nature. It points, as it were, to the vulnerability of the God who chooses to identify with human pain and suffering in the cross of Jesus of Nazareth. The crucified God, articulated in the theology of Jürgen Moltmann, is crucially linked with the pain and anguish in the world. Such a realization, moreover, underscores the need for a continual dependence on the Holy Spirit who is leading us ever forward into truth. We have not yet arrived. There is more yet to be discovered, revealed and known. There is always more to God than we can think or imagine.

3 Poetic theology

Pastoral theologians have often found at the bedside of critically ill patients that categorical doctrinal statements are patently unhelpful to engage the person in the situation. At such times less direct language, such as is found in poetry and art, often brings an awareness of the sublime and enigmatic in more powerful ways. In the face of the human condition and in the light of the vulnerability of God, what we have is the language of poetry, which in symbols and evocative expressions seeks to point to the unimaginable and unthinkable. Propositions may not be as helpful as poetry to express the reality of God and the ephemeral character of human experience. This language is imaginative, creative, playful and expressive. Pastoral encounter continually points in this direction. Pastoral theologians call us to an imaginative and creative place where the presence of the divine is approached very much as such presence is often encountered – in the silence, the absence, the pain unspeakable. Pastoral theologians point towards the subtlety and elusiveness of God's presence, because that is their experience and encounter in their practice. Pastoral theologians call those whose faith is shaped exclusively by texts into the light, reality and messiness of experience-in-the-world, where formulaic constructions too often fail to encompass or include particular cases.

In a collection of letters addressed to one of his grandchildren, Michael Wilson, medical officer during the Second World War and later in West Africa, Anglican priest, pioneering lecturer in pastoral studies at Birmingham University, offers a series of thoughtful explorations of issues such as prayer, unemployment, suffering and global justice (Wilson, 1995). Wilson encourages us towards maturity in the following words: 'Growing towards maturity, both as an individual and as a society means learning to hold together the good and the bad, love and fear, self-sacrifice and selfishness, creativity and destructiveness, in one's self and in other people.'

In a telling reflection on this theme Wilson wrote the following poem, during a stay at the flat of a Jungian analyst in London, on the biblical story of Jacob's wrestling with God. The poem is entitled 'Jacob and the Angel':

A wide-eyed spectre stalked the night,
Evil, brutish, mad.
He found me, 'ere the dawn of day
Could save me from my plight.
My blood ran cold,
My joints unloosed, I fought with all my might.
Dumb with terror
Walk with fear
I saw him grow in height.

Each thrust of mine he parried straight
As one who knows me well.
His own shrewd blows I least expected;
Yet I seemed to sense my fate
As one who sees an unknown place,
Yet knows it seen before
In previous life or dreaming state.
Such inward fears
Grew monstrous
As my heart o'erbrimmed with hate.

Hour after hour we strove to kill
Engripped in mental fight,
Until my ebbing strength gave way:
Backwards forced, he broke my will,
I fell.
Swiftly he pounced
My soul with darkness to fulfil,
And as he stooped
I raised my head
And kissed him, then lay still.

As wind stirs waves upon the corn
Shudders shook his frame
O'ercome by power of powerlessness:
By stab of love his heart was torn –
Immortal wound
Thrust deep.
His shrinking image paled at dawn,
Faded, failed and broke.
I knew the shadow's strength my own
And lay at peace new born.

(Wilson, 1995, pp. 92–3)

In the spring of 1984 Wilson and his wife Jean, following a final visit with his sister Joan who was dying in a hospice, set off for home in Birmingham. Just north of Oxford they were involved in a four-car pile-up, initiated by an exhausted medical officer asleep at the wheel. Michael and Jean suffered horrific injuries, including badly damaged eyes, multiple broken bones, and numerous severe cuts. Wilson was unconscious for four days. For months there was the possibility of his losing all sight. He lost sight in one eye. After a year of numerous operations he was able to walk again with the aid of a walking stick. The second of his poems I quote was written a couple of years after this painful experience.

The Answer's No!

Heralding dawn
A song thrush is shot by a youngster for fun
O Maker of both
Could you not wobble the aim of a gun
For a song?

Two cars
Speed towards one another
Head on:
The driver of one is asleep.
O Patron Saint of drivers
Could you not nudge him awake
Just in time?

A tiny child
Chases a bouncing ball
Into the road.
Drinking driver brakes too late.
O Guardian Angel of battered body
Could you not trip a toddler
On the kerb?

(Wilson, 1995, pp. 107–8)

Theology, when it is expressed in evocative, imaginative, poetic and indirect language, challenges unreflective, detached faith and may inspire us into relationship with the mystery that lies at the heart of the universal experience of pain, uncertainty and faith.

Wilson's insight is salutary:

We learnt the hard way, that it is not realistic to believe that God will save you from what you are afraid of. What you are afraid of may very well happen to you, but you will then find there is nothing to fear. Is there an answer to

the problem of suffering? Yes. You yourself are the answer.
(p. 109)

4 Exploring God – experience as work in progress

Theology is a path of challenge, discovery and adventure.
To invite one to the theological task is often to embark on
an *apophatic* journey in which many mirages and illusions
appear. The apophatic tradition is one in which we recognize
what cannot be true of God. We realize in the face of reality
and reflection that God cannot be like that which is often
claimed. Then, through a *via negativa* we seek to journey
towards what is more likely the case in God. We come slowly
to recognize the mirages but continue the search for the pools.
God is the horizon which is ever ahead and against which perspectives are taken. As we change our location, the horizon
appears to change too. However, the horizon continues to be
our line of orientation, perspective and discernment.

Theologians need to take more seriously people's reports
and stories of religious and other experience in their formulations and reflections. To discover the God who is intimately
related to creation it is important that theologians look closely
at and examine all of human experience including that which
has heretofore been described as 'secular' or 'profane' rather
than sacred. Much of African life is imbued with a quality of
sacrality that eluded the intruding and colonial Europeans,
for example. As a result of their insistence upon their own
perception of the sacred being the only one admissible, they
robbed the world of an impulse and introduction to the God
of all creation who has not left 'himself' without a witness in
all of humanity. Footprints, so to speak, of God are strewn all
over the world. The pastoral theological insight concerning
the importance of deep and active listening would have made
significant theological difference in the theological encounter between Europe and the rest of the world in the age of
European expansionism. The challenge now exists for such
listening to be engaged in.

Listening to the experiences of others is in the very nature of pastoral theology. This is a radical affirmation of the nature of the God of all creation. God is to be approached through listening to the limits of our existence. The being of God is encountered deeply in the otherness of those who most differ from ourselves. These others may help us to perceive the Other with whom we wish to be related. In fact we are unable even to begin to be related to the Other precisely because we are looking for the same – for One like us. We look for and desire God to be 'like us' in significant ways and thus are cut off from that which lies beyond us. The theological word from pastoral theologians is: listen to the different, for in this listening you may begin to encounter the Other whom you seek.

5 Divine vulnerability: God as weak in the world

It appears that God typically chooses to be weak, vulnerable and silent in the world rather than display great and visible power and might. In 1 Corinthians 1.18–25 earthly power and wisdom are contrasted with divine power and wisdom. Paradoxically, divine power is made manifest in the crucifixion – the harrowing suffering and death of Jesus. Divine wisdom is declared through the 'foolishness of preaching' about this same crucifixion. The nature of the presence and power of God in the world appears to be diametrically opposed to the ways of the world. Pastoral care providers rarely encounter a God who displays 'signs and wonders' or great demonstrations of superlative power. In more cases than not sufferers find strength not to remove the cause of their trouble but rather to cope with it. The presence of God is not in brash and brazen displays of power. God's reality appears subtle and elusive. The vulnerability and softness of God speaks more loudly than many would wish.

The incarnation of the Suffering Servant in Christian terms is paradigmatic of the presence of God to which pastoral theologians point. God chooses to empty God's self, divesting

God's self of all glory, majesty and power in order to be present in the world. God decisively enters the world through the Son. As if to make plain the manner of God's presence in the world, at every point in the life of Jesus he chooses not to display supernatural power to get his own way. Instead he willingly chooses the less glamorous path, the road of humble service, the way of the cross. Luke 4.1–13 records the temptation of Jesus and sets out the choice between crude displays of magical power (turning stones into bread; throwing oneself down from the pinnacle of the Temple) and the way of suffering service. At each point of temptation Jesus chooses the path of suffering. On the cross, when the thief asks for the dramatic escape – 'if thou be the Christ save thyself and us' (Luke 23.39) – Jesus resolutely refuses to use the power he evidently has. This criminal's question goes to the crux of the matter. If you are the Messiah, the promised powerful redeemer, then it would be expected that you would use your enormous power and role in the divine plan to rescue yourself and others from trouble, danger and death. However, Jesus the Son makes plain that that is not the manner of God's presence and power in the world. Pastoral theologians know this all too well. The divine presence is not to be gauged by great acts of personal deliverance from trouble and death. In fact, in more cases than not, the presence of God is to be found in the face of untold trouble and death.

Paul had to learn that the 'thorn' in his flesh would *not* be taken away; that God's grace would be sufficient for him to bear the thorn throughout his life (2 Cor. 12.7–10). Paul had to learn the paradoxical truth that his strength is to be found in weakness. Pastoral theologians can multiply examples down through the ages of history where people of faith have found this to be the case. God chooses to be weak in order for strength to be made manifest.

A helpful traditional theological distinction in this regard is that between the 'immanent' God and the 'economic' Godhead. God revealed in the world (economic – ordering the household (*oikonomia*) of the world) can be distinguished from the being of God within God's own self (immanent). Pastoral theologians have learnt through observing experience and repeated practice that the 'economic' God – manifest in the world in Christ and the Spirit – as perhaps distinct from the 'immanent' (what God is in God's self) is weak, even vulnerable. I would argue though that there is communion between the economic and immanent God, and that God's way of being in the world is freely chosen and in accord with God's being within God's self. What this means is that the God with whom we relate, from a Christian perspective, freely chooses to be vulnerable in the world because both the choosing and that manner of being in the world are consistent with the nature of God.

This profound and perhaps radical truth invites us all to re-construct our understandings and articulations of the power and omnipotence of God. Perhaps our concepts of an all-powerful God are too full of anthropomorphic images of empire and conquering warlords. Perhaps our God is too much like the ruling, dominating overlord. Such images are deeply disturbing to pastoral theologians, for they mislead and distort our experience of God in the world and ultimately lead us along a quest that can only lead to frustration and loss of faith.

6 Theology as desire for God's elusive love

Theology expresses the desire and longing of love. There is an appropriate and creative uncertainty that lies at the heart of theological discourse. In Scripture we find the stories of peoples who in faith follow their dreams and vocations. They experience God as beyond and ahead of them. They journey on in fulfilment of the callings they receive, ever expressing their desire and longing for the God who calls.

Theological language is the language of doxology, of worship. The loss of spirituality in scholarly theological discourse is akin to the loss of soul in the quest for life. The language of the Psalms and the Wisdom literature, as also evident in the discourse of the mystics, is full of passion, uncertainty and longing. It expresses the relationship of love that exists between a seeker and her beloved. Far from being the language of conquest, domination and unquestioning allegiance, it demonstrates the experience that pastoral theologians encounter. Here the believer wishes to trust and finds questions. The realities that confront the seeker are such that she longs for clarity and finds only glimpses. Glimpses evoke more longing and desire. In all of these, God remains elusive and yet evocative. In the search lies the power of love. Faith and love together impel us forward in the quest for union with the Beloved. In place of the paralysing effect of dread in the quest for God we find the energizing effect of love and desire for relationship. This God is not fearsome and fearful. This God lures and entices, even seduces us to follow. As process theologians John Cobb (Cobb and Griffin, 1976) and Robert Mellert (1975) would argue, God lures the world forward towards new forms of realization, harmonies and contrasts. In worship we seek after this alluring, enchanting, seductive One. In prayer and worship we seek relationship rather than understanding. Our minds take us very far on this road. We must never lose our minds. However, with our hearts we embrace, relate and proceed even further.

7 Humanity in the image of God

Theologians examine and explore the nature of humanity precisely because in the human we believe we catch glimpses of the divine Creator. To affirm that humanity is created in the image of God is to affirm that we can discover something – by no means all – about God by attention to the creature. Because humans are by their very nature related to God, we discover reflections of God through encounter with the human in all its complexity and danger. Pastoral care providers plumb the depths of human woe as well as human strength. God is to be discovered in both. Even the most appalling circumstances of human violence and depravity may illuminate something of the divine. The strength that inspires a Nelson Mandela and a Martin Luther King Jr to faithful action in the face of unspeakable odds, bespeaks the tenacious reality of the God we seek to know.

The rediscovery through feminist, womanist, ecological and liberation theologies of the subjugated tradition within Christianity in which the image of God is seen as relational rather than as an essential character or trait of humanity, has done much to move us into a more humane appreciation of both the divine and the human. Larry Kent Graham's account of and reflections on the narratives of care among lesbians and gay men concludes with a truly enlightening discussion of the relational nature of the image of God (Graham, 1997, pp. 163–87). Graham helps us see that because God's being is 'being-with' characterized by love, we image God by loving. Imaging God is not so much possessing some characteristic (such as rationality) as being relationally, as God is.

Pastoral theologians have learned that, in the final analysis, it is the quality of relationship that facilitates healing. The grace of God manifest in effective pastoral care – which mediates coping, successfully traversing and transcending the issues that life throws at us – lies not in superior knowledge but rather in the nature of the therapeutic relationship. In effect what is becoming clear is that imaging God is a relational matter. God is to be found in the 'other-directed' relationships of love and care.

8 Embracing the mystery: the search for an enigmatic God

The task of the theologian includes finding aesthetically, philosophically and pragmatically appropriate ways of embracing mystery. Theology is not so much about solving problems as it is about finding the grace, strength and humility to embrace mystery. In the ancient biblical story of Job we are not given an answer to the problem of evil or suffering, nor are we offered any statement about the nature of God the Creator. In fact Job's three counsellors who attempted to present conventional wisdom were ineffective with Job and were later declared inaccurate by God.

The ancient heritage of Asian religious plurality is that of positively living with difference. God is the God of the other who will remain other in authentic difference. As French philosopher Emmanuel Levinas argues, Otherness, God's otherness, will not and cannot be subsumed into our sameness. Likewise, the otherness of other humans will not be overcome by assimilation into our likeness. God, in Martin Buber, remains the transcendent Other whose otherness can only be related to in the I–Thou fashion that establishes the personhood of both the one relating and the One related to. The passion of Levinas's ethical philosophy is directed against all attempts to 'totalize' and subsume the other into our selves. Levinas charges western philosophy with having failed appropriately to deal with difference. For him the only really appropriate way is to recognize and 'become responsible' for respectfully maintaining the 'otherness of the other'. All attempts to make the other conform to our self are blasphemous and destructive.

Pastoral theologians seek to radically respect this transcending otherness in God and affirm difference within the human family. Larry Kent Graham puts it well when he writes, 'God is big enough to let each entity be itself, rather than something else. So must we be, if we reflect God's love' (1997, p. 176). As such, 'to be in the *imago dei*, therefore, is to ferociously protect and tenderly cherish the uniqueness of each entity in the world, while seeking the conditions of justice in which each might be fulfilled' (p. 177).

9 God as Being-in-relation

God is relational and is to be encountered within the relational matrices of our human life. It is significant that all the anthropological terms that are used in reference to the nature of God are interpersonal. 'Father', 'Mother', 'Son', 'Grandparent', 'Spirit', 'Creator', 'Sustainer', 'Renewer' – these are all meaningless in the absence of relation. This would also be language that pastoral theologians would articulate as being in keeping with our practice. It appears that the images of significance and importance that wield influence for good and ill in our experience are most often experienced and expressed in relational terms. Relationship, rather than individual isolated subjectivity, is that which impacts us most. In point of fact it is the nature and manner of the relationships we have with 'significant' figures that influences our sense of health, wellbeing and selfhood. This is true developmentally as well as socially. It is not so much that we project our need for an 'almighty' caretaker upon a father in heaven – as Freud would argue – as that it seems that we as human beings are constitutionally 'programmed' to discover significance through relationships. Our earliest relationships are clearly with parents and other primary care-givers. Little wonder then that the nature of our sense of significance is influenced by this everyday experience.

Paul Fiddes argues that the Trinity is better seen as dynamic relationships, 'movements of relationship subsisting in one event' (2000, p. 36) rather than as three individuals who have relationships. That 'Father', 'Son' and 'Spirit' are movements of relationship that interpenetrate and exist within and among one another is the force of the perichoretic Trinity affirmed by eastern and western Christians. With these expressions of dynamism and interaction, many pastoral theologians find agreement, especially since they mirror and express reality as it is unearthed through pastoral psychotherapy.

10 Theology in the global community

To come to understand the God who said 'Let us make Humankind after our image' (Gen. 1.26) we must listen to many voices from many different places on God's earth. To come to grips with what is crucial about salvation we must recognize that 'God so loved the World that God gave . . .' (John 3.16).

Theology requires a global, pluralistic perspective. In creation we recognize a God whose wisdom is made manifest through diversity. In the aetiological story recorded in Genesis 11 God acts to diversify and extend the languages of humanity, as if to affirm the divine love for plurality. In Acts 2 – at the birth of the Church – the action of God the Holy Spirit was to enable the gathered disciples to speak the languages of the known world, as if again to affirm the divine love of diversity. In these decisive acts of God recorded in both Testaments, we have the action of God directed at promoting or intensifying diversity. It is not far-fetched to say that God acts in history to create, affirm or re-establish diversity. Diversity is God's norm.

African notions of God as communal unity lead us to an understanding of nature and humanity as essentially communal. Interpersonal and corporate dimensions assume as great importance as the intra-personal. As pastoral theologians trained within the individualistic structures of the modernist and postmodernist West encounter more communal cultures they begin to realize the power of the communal for both good and ill. African flexibility and pliability in the face of the unrelenting onslaught of western imperialism, colonialism and slavery has been a survival art for Africans in the diaspora. Pastoral theologians who have given attention and care to the experiences of Africans on the continent and in the diaspora recognize and argue for the recognition of the plurality that lies at the heart of the unity of God. They would affirm as a result of this reflection that no one person, people, tradition or nation can claim monopoly on truth. God is communal. There is plurality and real difference in God. Theology is a corporate, indeed global matter.

Pastoral theologians do have a crucial theological contribution to make in church, academy and world community. A significant aspect of this contribution lies, as we have sought to do in this chapter, in presenting and discussing views concerning the nature of God and the interaction between the divine and the human as they have emerged through pastoral encounter. In the final chapter, which follows, the outworking of these theological considerations through pastoral reflections in different parts of the world and through varied experiences of persons within communities will be explored.

Questions for further exploration

1   To what extent do you agree with the assertion that pastoral encounters teach theology?
2   Describe and examine the nature of theological discourse that appears to you as you study this chapter.
3   How would you characterize or describe God on the basis of the reflections in this chapter?
4   How would you characterize or describe humanity on the basis of the reflections in this chapter?
5   Outline your understanding of and examine your responses to each of the ten assertions in the chapter.

5

Pastoral Theology at Work in the World

Critical, interpretive, constructive and expressive reflection on God's care and that of human communities has implications for the discipline of theology, the Church and the world community. As we have seen, notions concerning the nature of God influence, and are influenced by, the experiences and practices of pastoral care. In the Gospels the injunction to 'love one's neighbour as oneself' is closely linked in the teaching of Jesus to that of 'loving God with all one's mind, strength and heart'. The Church as the Body of Christ in the world manifests its theological insights most clearly by the ways it relates within itself and with the world community around it. As such, the practices of care, the love of God and the witness of faith within the world are inseparably linked. The question then becomes how this link may be examined and made manifest. This chapter explores the implications of the linkage of faith and practice that we have been calling 'pastoral theology' for the world community.

Changing paradigms

In exploring the link between pastoral care, pastoral theology and the life of faith within the world it is important first to point out a number of significant changes that have occurred, especially over the past century, in the reigning paradigms in pastoral care and pastoral theology. The models indicate what is involved in the reflective practices of care in the world.

These models are evident to differing degrees in different parts of the world and are helpful in understanding the nature of the practices of pastoral theology and pastoral care in each particular area of the world.

Historically four paradigms have been recognized (see Ramsey (ed.), 2004; Patton, 1993). In reality, these models co-exist, in some places in equal measure while in others one or other clearly has primacy. As such, though I shall be presenting them in chronological sequence in the order of each one's recognition and naming, it needs to be borne in mind that the emergence of a new paradigm does not mean the disappearance of the old. Moreover, the existence of one does not imply the absence of another.

Chronologically the earliest is a *classical-clerical* paradigm, in which the reflective practices of pastoral theology are implemented from start to finish by ordained members of the clergy. The discipline is clergy-led and clergy-focused. The practice is understood firmly and strongly as religious practice and the expert, if not the sole, practitioners are recognized, licensed or ordained clergy in their respective traditions. In Roman Catholic and Orthodox circles worldwide this model is paramount. Although lay pastoral care and counselling is increasingly recognized in the USA, the classical-clerical model continues to exert influence, not least because most programmes of training in pastoral theology require an academic qualification at masters level (for example, the M.Div) – the degree of choice for people aspiring to ordained ministry – and/or 'good standing' with a community of faith. Similarly in Africa, Latin America and Asia this model continues to play an important role although the communal nature of these societies means that it is manifest in a different way from that in more individualistic societies.

The clerical paradigm has been criticized especially in western European circles as individualistic, patriarchal, encouraging magical thinking, promoting dependence, and having an intrinsic tendency towards the abuse of power. Theologically it is seen as allied to a monarchical view of

God that can and has been associated with oppressive, paternalistic, imperialistic and colonial practices. Moreover, it is recognized that pastoral care is more often communally and unofficially ministered through the agency of lay people – and frequently women – whose ministry is not formally recognized or licensed.

A second paradigm emerged in the wake of sustained critique of the classical clerical one, and as a direct result of the growth of the human sciences, particularly psychology. This has been described as the *clinical-pastoral* paradigm. The reigning philosophies of this model are drawn from the medical and psychological disciplines. Here, the practices of pastoral theology and care are shaped by theories and practices of psychotherapy. Training for practitioners is in both theology and psychology. Clinical education for pastoral care is hospital-based and draws much of its theoretical and practical material from that context. In Europe and within liberal Protestant circles in the USA this model is mainstream. It has had such widespread influence that for some pastoral practitioners it is the only valid expression of pastoral care. Its presuppositions of dialogue and integration between theology and psychology shaped training within the disciplines of pastoral care and pastoral theology for many in this field in the twentieth century.

Next in order emerged what has been described as the *communal-contextual* model. This approach reacts against the clericalization, clinicalization and individualization of pastoral care and pastoral theology. Practitioners employing this model seek to restore these disciplines to their roots within communities of faith. It is communal because it challenges individualism and encourages communal and ecclesial formation and practice. The church as a relational and corporate community is both the base and the agent of care. Communities of faith are the loci of pastoral care and pastoral theology properly understood and practised. The 'clientele' is also communal – whole communities become the focus of pastoral strategies. It is contextual because it pays much more attention to the historical, social and cultural contexts of the communities that mediate pastoral care. It argues that attention needs to be paid to the wider social environment for effective care of persons to occur. Pastoral theologian Karen Scheib identifies four interconnecting and mutually reinforcing core values that inform this model:

1 Relationality and community are central.
2 Human development is a relational process which occurs within a social context.
3 Individual differences and cultural diversity are highly valued.
4 Mutuality and reciprocity are the hallmarks of the practices of pastoral care. (Scheib, 2002, p. 31)

The fourth is an emergent model, the *intercultural* paradigm, which extends the communal-contextual into a global nexus and asks questions concerning issues of global justice specifically including matters of race, gender, class, sexuality and economics. Its intercultual ethos expresses a 'non-reductive, open, creative and tolerant hermeneutics' (Mall, 2000, p. 6) which is democratic in a global sense and argues that wisdom does not belong only to one group, race, ideology or faith. This approach is polylingual, polyphonic and polyperspectival. Many voices need to be spoken, listened to and respected in our quest for meaningful and effective living. On the intercultural route all totalizing structures and systems are critiqued and challenged in recognition of the complexity, plurality, fragmentation and pluriformity of our postmodern and post-colonial times. According to philosopher Ram Mall, whose heritage is both Indian and German, 'intercultural philosophy as an open, tolerant, and pluralistic attitude consists of the philosophical conviction that the one philosophia perennis is the possession of no single culture or philosophical tradition' (Mall, 2000, p. 9).

Interculturality stands for an attitude that rejects both extreme relativism and exclusive absolutism. It inhabits different cultures but also seeks to transcend their narrow limits. The intercultural paradigm is increasingly influencing the pastoral disciplines through many avenues, not least encounters across cultures, social groups, religious faiths, gender and sexualities.

Pastoral theology is currently engaged within a global context in which all four paradigms are operative. Each has strengths and weaknesses. The challenge is to draw appropriately and contextually on them in the midst of a world of tensions, ambiguities and complexities.

Global tensions

The multicultural world scene within which pastoral theologians work is one of numerous dialectical tensions. The global scene is characterized by several questions that cannot simply be spoken of as evident in bipolar opposites. It is increasingly being realized that many of these issues overlap and complexify what were previously perceived in binary fashion. The particular questions and tensions I highlight below are also manifest within the practices of pastoral theology within our multicultural world. How can we be respectful of the *individual* and the *community* in ways that affirm both? What will be entailed in paying close attention to both the *intra-psychic* experiences of persons and the network of *interpersonal* relations within which they are embedded? In today's world the challenge of care is how to respond to people's *emotional* as well as their *economic* circumstances. Are we to be drawn towards the various expressions of *religion* or to the opportunities and ambiguities of *spirituality* as it is called upon in many societies today? With the scarce resources available or allocated to health care in many national budgets across the world shall we give greater attention to the eradication of *disease* through increasingly advanced technologies and therapeutic strategies or to the promotion of *health* through primary health care and public health education? With a virtual destruction of any alternatives in terms of 'superpowers', where shall we find our models of life and care – from the increasingly dominant *western* or else some kind of *global* perspectives that include indigenous, so-called 'Third World' knowledge? In our theologies do we continue to emphasize and study the *verbal* and *literary* expressive or do we give place to *aesthetic*, *non-verbal* expressive forms? In the face of increasing extremism, terrorism and violence emanating from identifiable sectors of the world community is it possible to make a sensible choice between radical *relativism* and absolute *essentialism*?

Intercultural pastoral theology: living in the tension

Pastoral theology spoken of in this book bears a significant theological insight in mind in addressing these questions from an intercultural point of view. Pastoral theologians are convinced that truth and good practice lie in the tension between opposing positions. As we have argued with respect to the relationship between 'theory' and 'practice', collapsing these tensions into one or other pole loses the importance that each contributes to the whole. In line with the intrinsic creative tension that lies at the heart of pastoral theology, the global task of the pastoral theologian is to maintain these tensions in creative and imaginative ways, recognizing that truth lies not at one extreme pole in opposition to the other, but rather in maintaining the contributions of seemingly divergent poles. The deadly logic of 'either–or' privileges one pole to the exclusion, suppression or annihilation of the other. Such thinking often lies at the root of the extremism and intolerance about which we are all exercised at this current juncture in world history.

The Christian theological construction of the Trinity as we have seen illustrates the maintenance of tensions within a tri-polar reality. Pastoral theologians affirm this unity-in-diversity as also evident in human experience. The pastoral theological task – and it is a crucial one in the twenty-first century – is to assist in the formation of persons and communities that are adept at living creatively and constructively within the tensions and extremes of life. Conflict as a result of religious convictions and differences marred the life of the world in the twentieth century. The scourge of the twenty-first century appears to be violence and terrorism in the name of and by the conviction, no matter how erroneous or misconstrued, of religion. Faith-inspired violence to self and others has assumed terrifying proportions. Political and national responses to violence that in turn invoke other religious and ideological reasons for acts of further violence and war, make matters no better. There is a pastoral theological response that is called for in the current international dilemma. It has to do with living creatively *with* extremes rather than *by* extremes. It is a way of respectful living; a way of peace-with-justice; a way of non-violent activism.

In an important summary article on 'Gender as construct and category in pastoral theology', North American pastoral theologian Nancy Gorsuch identifies the shift in the literature from 'categorical, biologically-based sexual difference to gender as ambiguous social construct' (Gorsuch, 2000, p. 108). This more fluid view of gender, she acknowledges, does not mesh with the concrete experiences of many women in families, communities and nations where the reality is more 'rigid, fixed and categorical'. How do we move communities, societies, religious traditions, even nations towards a more graceful and care-filled place? This precisely is the challenge for pastoral theologians and other practical theologians whose vocation is to care within God's creation. Gorsuch's review of the pastoral theological literature and practice leads her to the hopeful comment that 'pastoral theologians are finding a way to explore gender difference without reinforcing opposition or stabilizing notions of essential nature, and doing so through careful attention to the ambiguity of gender in human experience' (p. 108).

At the heart of the dilemma and danger of our multicultural world lies the central issue of how to live respectfully with difference and ambiguity. The crucial central question in the world today, in my view, is the following: *How are persons of different ethnicities, cultures, genders, faiths and socio-economic circumstances to live together reasonably on one earth, the resources of which are not unlimited, in the light of historic relations of dominance and subjugation?*

Otherness, selfhood and the 'enigmatic relation': difference in an intercultural world

Kojo (38) had been distressed for several years before he was referred to me by a psychiatric social worker. The diagnostic label that had been given him by the psychiatrist was 'paranoid schizophrenic'. Kojo's father was the director, before retirement, of a large scientific research institution. His mother was a high-school teacher. Kojo was the eldest of three children. He had a sister and brother. All, apart from his father, who described himself as agnostic, were active in church. Kojo had completed high school successfully and entered university to read sociology. He had dropped out in his second year. Before he had withdrawn completely into an almost impenetrable shell, Kojo had been a worship leader and reader in the church. In spite of encouragement from several professionals, Kojo flatly refused to come to see me. His social worker had thought that given the similarity of our ethnic origins and also religious faith that he would have found interactions with me more helpful than intrusive. 'I told him you were a Christian psychotherapist and a professor of theology from his own country,' she wrote to me, 'I expect that will be encouraging to him.'

After several months I decided, in full awareness of the breech of certain professional codes involved in this, to make a pastoral visit and go to look Kojo up. On my first two visits Kojo refused to see me. On the third, he came out and for the first time sat with me for 20 minutes. He was mostly non-communicative, responding in monosyllables and incomplete phrases. Over the next several sessions we began to develop the beginnings of what might be described as an acquaintance. We began to be able to carry on a conversation for a few minutes at a time.

I believe it was the eighth time we met that Kojo made the startling comment, 'I am sure you are a snake, like the rest of them.' (In the following account C = me, K= Kojo.)

C: Tell me more about snakes.

K: Well, they are pretty dangerous.

C: How?

K: They, well, they . . . that is the venomous boa constrictors have a lethal effect on their victims. (Wow, this is much more than I have ever heard Kojo say.)

C: And then?

K: Then what? (He's certainly communicative.)

C: Well, tell me more about what snakes do to their victims.

K: (After a long pause.) They paralyse the victims with the spray they spit out at them and then when they are incapacitated they begin to swallow them whole.

C: Tell me what makes you think I am like a snake.

K: Over the last six years of my life I have been passed from one professional to the next. I have been drugged and medicated 'for my own good', to make me feel better, to stimulate me, but all I have felt is more paralysed and trapped.

C: Huh huh.

K: Yes, and now you come along . . . with your long words and confusing talk . . . which also only does my head in – the effect is the same. I am trapped. And when you are finished with me there will be nothing left of me.

C: How so?

K: Come on . . . you professors, professionals, social workers are all the same. You paralyse us and then you swallow us up. Some of you do it physically with medications, others – like you – with your labels and 'diagnosis'. They told you I was 'paranoid' didn't they? And now you are in the process of verifying that. The label is all you see. I am not a person to you, I am a case, a category. You have already swallowed me up in your diagnosis!'

As I have pondered a response to the central question of our multicultural world, the thinker who has had the greatest impact and relevance for my thoughts has been philosopher Emmanuel Levinas (1906–95). In a series of publications spanning a period of over 65 years Levinas left a legacy that has gone far beyond his primary discipline of philosophy. Born of Jewish parents in Lithuania in 1906, Levinas moved to France in 1923. He later studied under the great phenomenologists Husserl and Heidegger, in Freiburg, Germany, between 1928 and 1929. Phenomenology was the name Husserl gave to his philosophical method of paying attention to what can be seen and describing it as clearly and accurately as possible, without presuppositions or deductions from general principles. Phenomenology was essentially an intuitive art.

Levinas earned his doctorate as a phenomenologist and is credited in his early work with making phenomenology better known in France, influencing the existentialism of Jean-Paul Sartre and Maurice Merleau-Ponty. After serving as the director of a Jewish school, Levinas received his first university appointment. Following years at the universities at Poitiers and Nanterre, he was appointed in 1973 Professsor of Philosophy at the Sorbonne.

The most significant aspects of Levinas's work emerge out of his dissatisfaction with the phenomenology of Husserl and Heidegger. Following the Second World War Levinas's initial concerns with the ethical dimension of philosophy – especially the ethical nature of the relation between the Self and the Other – come to dominate his work. His philosophy came to revolve around the one decisive and far-reaching theme – a concern that western philosophy has consistently practised a suppression of the Other.

The importance of Levinas's work for pastoral theologians in our multicultural world derives from the crucial role it gives to the issue and problem of 'otherness'. Working with the terms 'Same' (or Self) and 'Other', introduced into philosophical debate by none else than Plato, Levinas pursues an account of the relationship between Same and Other which has been very influential in French and latterly much of European thinking. Levinas's work is complex and difficult to understand. It is nevertheless very rewarding and illuminating of what to me remains *the* central issue in our multicultural world.

Levinas is concerned that the Other in western thought has tended to be seen as only temporarily different from the Self; that, given time, education or development, the Other would come to be as the Self. British scholar Colin Davis puts it well when he writes:

> In Levinas's reading of the history of Western thought, the Other has generally been regarded as something *provisionally separate* from the Same (or the self), but ultimately reconcilable with it; otherness, or alterity, appears as a temporary interruption to be eliminated as it is incorporated into or reduced to sameness. (Davis, 1996, p. 3, emphasis mine)

Davis continues:

> For Levinas, on the contrary, the Other lies absolutely beyond my comprehension and should be preserved in all its irreducible strangeness . . . Levinas attempts to protect the Other from the aggressions of the Same, to analyse the possibilities and conditions of its appearance in our lives, and to formulate the ethical significance of the encounter with it. (p. 3)

This attempt to respectfully maintain the otherness of the Other and the integrity of the Self, while also working out an ethical way of being in relation with the Other is, in my view, the dilemma of the age. It is a dilemma stalking the corridors of power and the multicultural streets of London, Paris, Amsterdam, New York, Sydney and Toronto in the twenty-first century.

Levinas's voluminous works illustrate this struggle. In *Time and the Other* (1987, originally published in 1947) Levinas explores the nature of human existence in terms of relationship with the Other. In contrast to Hegel, Levinas insists on the irreducibility of the Other. The significance of this in pastoral theology lies in the high view held of the integrity of the Other and the insistence that all attempts, both subtle and overt, to create or construe the other as being 'in my image' are futile and costly. In *Totality and Infinity* (first published in 1961) Levinas challenges what he sees as a dangerous drive to unity and unification that leads to a closed, inevitably destructive system of totality that has characterized western philosophy – ultimately expressed in the Holocaust. In political terms there is an important point being emphasized. The power that drives groups and nations to seek unification is self-destructive if it does not enable respect for difference. The imagery of the 'Melting Pot' in which all are reduced to a sameness as 'Americans' while still having some relevance in national, legislative and political terms has proved to be unworkable in cultural, linguistic and many other senses.

In *Otherwise than Being or Beyond Essence* (1974), Levinas re-orients the subject, the Self, the person, arguing that it is not Being but *being otherwise*, directing oneself towards the Other, that is the prior reality constituting a self. It is in being oriented towards the other that the Self finds its own identity. This orientation towards the Other is the driving force of *agape* love and pastoral care.

Levinas disagrees with Husserl's description (following Leibniz) of the Self as monad, self-contained and isolated from other monads. For Husserl each monad mirrors all others, so that although I cannot see or touch the monadic Ego of the Other, the very fact that I call it monadic implies that it is in important respects similar to my own. For Husserl, the Other can be known by empathy (*Einfühlung*): not because I can cast off my own Self, but because all Egos reflect each other. The Other, Husserl would argue, is a reflection of myself, and because each Ego is a monad, reflecting, containing and contained in all other Egos, then community, communion, empathy, harmony and reciprocal recognition are possible. These intersubjective relations are all possible because all Egos reflect all others.

Pastoral counselling that follows Object Relations Theory is similar to Husserl's views because it too is premised on processes of internalization in which the 'Other' is understood, subsumed, accessed and responded to through internal objects. Although the Other is never fully present to me, he or she is known by empathy and assimilated because conceived as a reflection of myself. Levinas finds this entirely unsatisfactory. In Levinas's view, Husserl's attempt to demonstrate the existence of transcendental Egos other than my own in effect leaves no place for the Other as Other. It actually does violence to the Other because it crushes and re-creates her or him in my image. In my interactions with Kojo one thing was painfully clear: he experienced professionals as working hard to 'swallow him up' into their labels and thus reduce him to themselves through their categories. The image of the snake that swallows its victim whole was what Kojo chose to use to describe this mechanism.

It is significant that Heidegger also rejects Husserl's notion of empathy as a key to understanding the Other. Empathy, Heidegger would argue, implies that the Other is merely a kind of duplicate of the Self and therefore an inherent part of the Being. So Heidegger sets out in his work to resist the reduction of alterity brought about, in his view by Husserl's phenomenology. In Heidegger's account the world is shared with others – the prefix *mit* ('with') is crucial for Heidegger. The world of *Dasein* is a *Mitwelt* ['with-world']. Being-in the world is Being-with [*Mitsein*] Others.

Heidegger's account has many attractions for Levinas because the others with whom *Dasein* shares the world are *not* conceived of as reflections of myself. So far so good. How-ever, what worries Levinas marks him off as what I would describe as a 'practical' (even pastoral) philosopher-cum-theologian. It is that Heidegger's ontological concerns off-set this important gain because he is interested in 'modes of Being rather than empirical encounters' (Davis, 1996, p. 29). As in Object Relations Theory the actual empirical presence of others is irrelevant for Heidegger. This is precisely why Levinas disagrees. For Levinas,

the other is in no way another myself, participating with me in a common existence. The relationship with the other is not an idyllic and harmonious relationship of communion or a sympathy through which we put ourselves in the other's place; we recognize the other as resembling us, but exterior to us; the relationship with the other is a relationship with a Mystery. (Levinas, 1987, p. 75)

Thus Levinas insists on real life encounters with real people as the only true means of genuine knowledge. Intercultural encounter is a means of real growth, knowledge and care.

Further to reflect this sense of mystery that is central to otherness, Levinas engages in reflections on death. He argues that things occur that are not always already intended and known by the transcendental Ego or assumed within the relationship with Being. The Other (for example, death, text, person) is encountered as an essential mystery; it is not known or knowable. In his 1965 essay, 'Enigme et phenomene', Levinas begins to develop what he calls a *philosophy of the enigma*, rather than a philosophy of the phenomenon which appears in the light as an object of (my) knowledge. He develops a philosophy of darkness in which the Other is never fully seen, known or possessed. Rather than seeking knowledge of the Other (thus reducing its otherness) we should accept that we do not, cannot and should not know the Other. Levinas's career came then to be dominated by one question: What does it mean to think of the Other as truly Other?

This question and its implications are for me as a therapist and pastoral theologian the crux of all intercultural, indeed all pastoral, encounters and therapy. How can I relate critically, crucially and responsibly with Others in a way that respects and preserves their authenticity as Other? In what is one of the most quoted passages of Levinas's *Totality and Infinity*, he describes the essence of his ethical approach:

A calling into question of the Same – which cannot occur within the egoistic spontaneity of the Same – is brought about by the Other. We name this calling into question of my spontaneity by the presence of the Other ethics. The strangeness of the Other, his irreducibility to the I [Moi], to my thoughts and my possessions, is precisely accomplished as a calling into question of my spontaneity, as ethics. (p. 43)

The Other puts me into question by revealing to me that my powers and freedom are limited. In the face-to-face encounter, the Other gives my freedom meaning because I am confronted with the real choices between responsibility and obligation towards the Other, or hatred and violent repudiation. Thus the relationship between the Same and Other – two authentic, irreducible selves – has become the site where both ethics and knowledge are at stake. It is such relationship, in which Self and Other remain authentic and irreducible, that is necessary in our multicultural world.

The central problem for Levinas was to elaborate a philosophy of Self and Other in which both are preserved as independent, self-sufficient and authentic, but also in some sense in relation with one another. This is more difficult than might appear, since it is in the nature of relations to bring the Other into the Self's sphere of familiarity, thus making it intelligible from the perspective of the Self and thus reducing its true otherness, 'because knowledge is always *my* knowledge, experience always *my* experience; the object is encountered only in so far as it exists *for me*, and immediately its alterity is diminished' (Davis, 1996, p. 41). To preserve the Other as Other, it must not become an object of knowledge or experience; Levinas is concerned to preserve the authenticity of the Other and not to diminish it in any way. As such he sought an account of alterity which does not reduce the Other to the Same and a means of accounting for the relation between Same and Other that does not effectively abolish either.

Like Descartes who observed that the infinite must necessarily remain beyond the understanding of finite beings such as myself, Levinas argued that this essential lack of intelligibility also characterizes the Other when viewed from the standpoint of the Self. Indeed for Levinas the failure of understanding is essential if the radical otherness of the Other is to be preserved. The difficulty in describing the encounter with alterity lies in the constant danger of transforming the Other, however unwittingly or unwillingly, into a reflection or projection of the Self.

Levinas maintains that it is in face-to-face encounter that truth is established. For Levinas truth, knowledge and justice are not attained in solitary thought but rather in face-to-face conversation with the Other. Truth involves a direct engagement in ethics, which starts with a basic act such as engaging in dialogue with the Other. Levinas uses the analogy of the 'face of the Other' to pursue this dialogical direction. To know truth is to recognize that the face of the Other limits and prohibits injustice. To practise truth is to welcome the Other. The face of the Other resists possession and invites one into an ethical relationship of responsibility. What occurs in the epiphany of the face is that I am invited to ethical responsibility. In stressing exteriority over interiority, dialogue and welcome over totality, Levinas argues that the Other invites the Same to responsibility.

Robert Gibbs writes:

> Levinas' phenomenology climaxes in the moment I am face to face with another person. The face is the experience that lies at the root of ethics for Levinas . . . My obligation to be for the other rests in his human face, not as a cluster of nose and eyes, etc., but as announcement of my responsibility for him . . . The separation between the other and myself is an inassimilable difference proclaimed in the other's face. I cannot make him mine, nor reduce him to my cognition of him. (Gibbs, 1992, p. 165)

What Levinas achieves, then, as feminist biblical scholar Tamara Eskenazi puts it, is the construction of a 'relational self based on connectivity *that values difference*' (Eskenazi, 2003b, p. 148, my emphasis). He constructs an ethical, relational Self that preserves the integrity of the Other and does not presume to either dominate or assimilate such Other. Eskenazi writes:

Like several important feminists, Levinas reconstitutes the subject, exploring how we best understand the subject without succumbing to essentialism or constructing the other on the basis of the same and in antagonism toward it. Since woman in Western religion and philosophy has been, as de Beauvoir has shown, the paradigmatic other, the revaluation of the Other in Levinas invites feminist appreciation and appropriation. It is therefore not surprising that several feminists acknowledge their indebtedness to Levinas. (Eskenazi, 2003b, p. 150)

Levinas constitutes a subject – a Self – on the model of connectivity, rather than the dominant separatist object/subject Self. He opposes the fusing of normative western traditions with one that does not merge/assimilate the Other into oneself or recast the Other in categories of the Same but remains, instead, in a relation of responsibility. Derrida's expression of an 'enigmatic relationship' between Self and Other remains for me the most significant way of describing relations between them in which there is authenticity, integrity and difference. What lies at the heart of the intercultural encounter that we have been proposing is not an easy, optimistic gliding over differences in a soppy tolerance that superficially embraces and shakes hands with smiling 'alterns'. Rather it is the difficult, respectful, dangerous and enigmatic encounter between autonomous, different but integrated persons self-aware and vulnerable in their full humanity.

From a Levinasian perspective, then, since selfhood is constituted by an ethical relation of responsibility to the Other, it is our task as pastoral theologians to do all in our power to preserve the otherness of the Other as well as seek to promote 'enigmatic relationships' (à la Derrida) between persons of difference. This will entail, in pastoral theology, a resolute refusal to define/interpret the Other on my own terms alone. Implied in this will be a respectful and humble acknowledgement of not knowing – indeed of the ultimate unknowability of our partners. The Other will for ever remain a mystery, but a mystery to be embraced in relationship. In this relationship the Other is allowed complete freedom to define themselves and speak for themselves on their own terms. For this to be realized in reality, power differentials of the most subtle sort will need to be recognized. Such power differences exist along economic, social, psychological, religious and on many other lines. Then we must face them squarely through open acknowledgement and discussion. Thus pastoral theology in our multicultural world involves the risky business of travelling alongside the Other in the quest for true selfhood for us all.

This way of framing selfhood and otherness, nevertheless, is premised on a decidedly western post-Enlightenment concept of selfhood that upholds the notion of discrete, unitary individuals. African notions of personhood, for example, are far more communal. Here individuals are not discrete and unitary but rather participate in the very otherness we have been describing in crucial ways that do not negate or subsume them. To African thinking the person is a community of selves in community with others.

My pastoral counselling work with Kojo took a turn for the better when we began to work with his views and images. Slowly he began to realize that I was not out to prove anything nor to make him into some preconceived 'healthy self'. He began to relax when I encouraged him, in different ways, to speak in his own way on whatever he felt and when he became convinced that I was not wedded to any diagnostic label. My aim was to permit Kojo to be the 'Other' he was without subsuming or accommodating him to me or my reality. What emerged was a fascinating array of images of himself. Kojo-the-storyteller, Kojo-the-dreamer, Kojo-the-spirit, Kojo-the-reincarnated one, were all allowed to talk to each other and to me. I was brought face to face not with *an*-other, but rather with *many*-others. This was not a discrete unit but a community of related selves, overlapping without subsuming one another.

Kojo volunteered the fact that his alienation from the

church had been sealed when a church leader had diagnosed him as demon-possessed. Now here on the other hand was I, a church person who would allow his 'many selves' to talk with each other without labelling him as either 'schizophrenic' or demon-possessed. Secular professionals had a label for his behaviour. Ecclesial professionals also had their own spiritual terminology and label for him. Little wonder that Kojo was so distrustful of professionals. My view was that neither of these labels was sufficient. All were simplistic and reduction-istic, leaving him in his fullness and complexity out of the picture. Worse still, they were ways of comprehending Kojo entirely in terms of the one who did the labelling – the Self or Same of western philosophy. Working with Kojo enabled me to gain some insight into African personhood as communi-tarian through and through.

Personhood: the individual-in-community

The existence of Africans in the Caribbean and North America serves as an example of the complexities of relations between humans in history, differing understandings of personhood, and the practices of faith in the world. The institution by Europeans of slavery on the basis of race, its historic aboli-tion and the ongoing consequences of its aftermath evidenced in segregation, racism, patterns of inequality, privilege and domination, the problematics of identity, self-hatred, nihilism and violence highlight a grave human predicament. Colonial-ism had a similar if less obvious effect. To be civilized one had to be absorbed into the world and frame of the Self. As African American womanist scholar Barbara Holmes points out, communal responses to the collective context of oppres-sion on the part of the African American community did not pay sufficient attention to the devastating long-term personal effects of oppressive and institutionalized racism. As a result many African Americans still struggle with issues of identity (Holmes, 2002, p. 18).

W. E. B. du Bois in 1903 uncannily expressed a reality that

itinues to frame a struggle that western civilization has by
d large been unable to resolve. These postmodern times
sharpen the dilemma as the deep ambivalence concerning
selfhood and the meta-narratives of western history continue
to tantalize. Du Bois wrote of the 'Negro experience of double
consciousness' as follows:

> the Negro is a sort of seventh son, born with a veil, and
> gifted with second-sight in this American world, – a world
> which yields him no true self-consciousness, but only lets
> him see himself through the revelation of the other world.
> It is a peculiar sensation, this double-consciousness, this
> sense of always looking at one's self through the eyes of
> others, of measuring one's soul by the tape of a world that
> looks on in amused contempt and pity. One ever feels his
> twoness, – an American, a Negro; two souls, two thoughts,
> two unreconciled strivings; two warring ideals in one dark
> body, whose dogged strength alone keeps it from being torn
> asunder. (Du Bois, 1989, p. 5)

Barbara Holmes, more recently, helps us realize that it is even
more complex than the binary situation of double consciousness when she writes about 'multiple consciousness':

> Recent scholarship identifies the phenomenon not as
> double, but multiple consciousness. This is a complex
> state of being that includes fluctuating life perspectives.
> The term 'multiple consciousness' also recognizes the
> negotiated aspect of human interactions that include the
> varied accents contributed by gender, sexuality, race and
> class . . . We have yet to reintegrate fractured spirits and
> psyches, because we are only beginning to understand
> the personal consequences of oppression. (Holmes, 2002,
> pp. 18–19)

The African American pastoral theologian Homer Ashby
has recently helped us see within the African American community that the preacher, and indeed the Black Church as a

whole, has employed two significant forms of activity in their struggle for selfhood and in their ministry within the church and the community. These are 'conjuring' and 'signifying'. Conjuring evokes the activities of the traditional African priest-healer (erroneously referred to as a 'fetish priest' or 'witchdoctor') whose ritual arts were believed to bring healing to the community and ward off the harmful effects of evil. Ashby asserts: 'Conjuring was a means by which Africans brought to bear the power of transcendent forces to effect change in the this-world context. Conjuring produced healing, altered outcomes, precipitated reversals, and otherwise refashioned the course of events' (Ashby, 2003, p. 12).

Biblical stories, such as the Exodus in particular, have been 'conjured' by Africans in America to explain, translate and transform African American life. Of signifying, Ashby says:

> The signifying tradition is that form of African American cultural expression in which an indirect critical judgment is made about a person or circumstance. As a mode of rhetorical interpretation, signifying seeks to reveal or expose meanings and feelings that lie underneath words and actions. (p. 12)

Through conjuring and signifying, African American preachers, as recognized early by du Bois (1903) and commented upon by both Levine (1977, p. 58) and Harris (1995, p. 71), have sought to transform current circumstances and offer a critical perspective of hope and challenge for the future. Du Bois saw the connection of African American preachers to their African forebears, declaring the priest or medicine man the 'chief remaining institution' of the African past on the plantation. Du Bois writes:

> He early appeared on the plantation and found his function as the healer of the sick, the interpreter of the Unknown, the comforter of the sorrowing, the supernatural avenger of wrong, and the one who rudely but picturesquely expressed

the longing, disappointment, and resentment of a stolen
and oppressed people. Thus, as bard, physician, judge,
and priest, within the narrow limits allowed by the slave
system, rose the Negro preacher, and under him the first
Afro-American institution, the Negro church. (Du Bois,
1989, pp. 159–60)

The African American preacher then embodied – and to an
extent still does today – the mystical as well as the pragmatic concerns of the community in its quest for meaning
and transformative experience. The clerical function within
this community combines a charismatic leadership role with
a mystic-interpretive function that is embodied in the worship and the practices of faith of the community. The Black
preacher then embodies, conjures and signifies the pastoral
theologian of the community.

Dale Andrews helpfully points out the invidious influence
of individualism as a major problem in the dynamics of Black
religious life, as evidenced for example in the chasm between
the Black Church and Black theologians (Andrews, 2002).
Andrews deftly calls for a remarriage of the pastoral and the
prophetic strands within Black communal life through the
practice of liberative ethics in church and academy.

What is being expressed here is the search for and embodi-
ment of personhood. In African thought a person is a collective of individual, social and divine elements held together
through love, hope and meaning. Where this does not exist,
as Cornel West has described, there is a descent into nihilism.
In *Race Matters*, West uses the term to describe a horrific life
experience.

Nihilism is to be understood here not as a philosophic
doctrine that there are no rational grounds for legitimate
standards or authority; it is, far more, the lived experience of coping with a life of horrifying meaninglessness,
hopelessness, and (most important) lovelessness. The
frightening result is a numbing detachment from others

and a self-destructive disposition toward the world. Life without meaning, hope, and love breeds a coldhearted, mean-spirited outlook that destroys both the individual and others. (West, 1994, pp. 22–3)

A crucial task implied in our discussions of pastoral theology is precisely the facilitation of a life imbued with meaning, hope and love within the world community where persons' individuality and their sociality may flourish.

Widening the scope, increasing the depth

In parts of Africa, the classical-clerical model holds sway within different traditions. Reasons for this include the dearth of lay practitioners who are 'qualified' by western standards and, perhaps of greater significance, the fact that ordained clergy fulfil in many places the symbolic and overt role increasingly being vacated by the priest-healer in African traditional religion. The traditional African priest-healer's role has been under serious threat with the rise of first the Independent church prophet, later the Pentecostal preacher, and more recently the charismatic ministry founder and leader. The clergywoman or man, regardless of faith tradition, is seen as a representative and symbol of the transcendent in the midst of the community. An example of this occurred poignantly in my own life and ministry while I was serving as a chaplain in a high school in Accra, Ghana. A security officer in the school died on the day after he had received a pay rise. He was a Muslim, though not a strict one, since it was alleged with evidence that he died as a result of imbibing alcohol to excess. His family had no qualms in approaching the Christian school chaplain to perform his funeral rites and burial as an African Muslim. What was of greatest significance for all gathered was that a religious rite of burial was performed by a representative of the Divine presence, in which the name and blessing of God was sought for the deceased. This African sense of sacred community, connection of the living with the dead through

143

ritual performance by one seen as selected by the Divine, was pervasive and superseded the religious affiliation of both the deceased and the officiant. In this regard it is instructive that the Gospels portray Jesus as having much to say in commendation of the faith of non-Jews, including the oppressive Romans (for example, the Roman centurion in Luke 7.1–10), the Canaanite woman in Matthew 5.21–28, and the Samaritans despised by Jews especially because of their religion and ethnicity (for example, the Samaritan leper in Luke 17.11–19 who was the only one of the ten cured by Jesus to return and give thanks; and the 'good' Samaritan in Jesus' parable in Luke 10.30–36). Pastoral theologians are called upon to widen the scope of their theological discussions and practices. The God of all creation appears to summon theologians of all traditions into a dialogue about life. The burning question for me as a pastoral theologian in this situation was this: In the face of tragedy and grief what is my role within the community? What is more significant, doctrinal purity or relational wholeness?

The situation in Europe is very different, with clergy continually finding themselves marginalized along with the churches, in the political and social spheres of life, as their membership dwindles. The classical-clerical model here appears only largely where the clergy have been able to reinvent themselves as community activists, social workers, qualified therapists or educators. The clinical pastoral model fits well here, for the pastor becomes also a therapist. There is a widening of scope from the exclusively religious ritual function to a broadly therapeutic one open to all regardless of faith tradition.

In both the African and the European example then there is a broadening of scope. In the African it is an embrace of plurality of faith in the practice of care. In the European it is a broadening of function also in the service of care. I would argue that such a broadening actually results in greater depth. In the African situation I was forced to explore my Christian heritage and tradition even more deeply as I sought to discover ways of relating to my Muslim neighbours respectfully without abandoning my faith. I became more aware of the historic links and misunderstandings between these two great traditions. I was also able to focus more deeply on what was crucial in the mediating of care for the grieving family and to realize that our shared humanity was much deeper than our different persuasions of faith. Pastoral encounter with difference has the potential to deepen one's realization of essential matters.

Heart strings and purse strings

Increasingly pastoral theologians have had to broaden the scope of our discipline as we have recognized the devastating impact of social forces upon human life. The most recent examples in the pastoral theological literature come from experiences in Central and South America. North American pastoral theologian James Poling has helped us all appreciate this through his living, listening to and teaching in Nicaragua. His book *Render unto God* (2002) is an example of a new pastoral theology which includes careful economic analysis of the lives and living conditions of persons in poverty in different cultural contexts. He draws on a multitude of creative responses to political and socio-economic exploitation including by African Americans (pp. 123–41) and women (pp. 142–64). Poling finds in the African American celebration of Kwanzaa, and the formation of women's groups to challenge domestic, sexual and labour violence, powerful examples of resistance among underprivileged, powerless groups. He points to a spirituality of resistance and empowerment that infuses and invigorates all the activities of these particular groups of people. In all of this Poling calls for a transformation and revision of pastoral care and counselling so that they take into account the needs of persons in situations of family violence and economic vulnerability. In such situations, rather than individuals paying for pastoral care and counselling, the expenses of care are borne by the whole community. Care in these contexts follows a communal contextual model that seeks to make a real difference in the lives of the most economically vulnerable.

Pastoral theologians thus now call for attention to both heart strings and purse strings. The call is far-reaching for it envisages a fairly extensive change in the nature of the practices of care within a world that is driven by violence, from the most intimate, interpersonal contexts to the international and global.

United by multiple identities

Korean American theologian Andrew Sung Park has been a prolific and generative thinker about theological multiculturalism. Writing out of his own twin Korean and American heritages he seeks to engage in a theological dialogue that is respectful and critical of both heritages. His early work makes reference to the Korean and Vietnamese concept of *han*. Park shows how the traditional language of sin within Christian discourse has focused on the sinner to the neglect of the victim. He finds in the notion of *han* – the psychic and spiritual hurt, scars and pain of the victim of unjust oppression and suffering – language that helps in the development of a fuller doctrine or concepts of sin and redemption (Park, 1993). Park's integrative and dialogical work builds up a more nuanced and balanced view of the effects of human sin. By drawing on eastern and western thought, he shows how reflections on the experiences of the 'sinned against' and the 'sinner' are necessary in the formulation of any real understanding of human evil as well as ideas about redemption, healing and justification (Park, 2004). He also shows how fruitful a respectful dialogue between East and West, Asian and European can be in the development of Christian doctrine.

Park proposes a theology of enhancement as the key to multicultural living and growth. His vision is of different cultural groups working together to enhance each other's wellbeing.

Enhancement means to increase the beauty, worth, strength
or value of something. This enhancement model is an effort
to heighten the strengths, beauty, and value of racial and
ethnic groups by helping one another in growth. This
model envisions the enhancement of the cultural heritages
of diverse groups and the cooperation of each other in
transforming the shortcomings of each ethnic culture with
care. (Park, 2004, p. 16)

Park is clear that mutuality is crucial for enhancement and
transformation. His notion is not a naive sentimental celebration. He argues for transformation through internal as well
as mutual critique of the social and internal sin and *han* of
each group. Using the example of 'salt', he argues that 'in the
food, the grains of salt must lose their outer forms to perme-
ate it' (2004, p. 18). However, the salt must maintain its taste
to be of use. 'If we simply maintain our solitary form, we fall
into our own enclave. If we lose our form without keeping
our own taste we become merely assimilated to the dominant
culture' (2004, p. 18).

In what I consider to be an adept usage of concepts out
of Korean language and thought translated and interpreted
into Christian discourse, Andrew Sung Park urges Korean
Americans to move from an existential state of *han*, to an
essential state of *hahn*, *jung* and *mut*. These three interpen-
etrating and interconnected concepts inspire a multicultural
ethos in which mutual enhancement is possible. Park trans-
lates *hahn* as 'radical inclusiveness', an undivided whole,
Divine supremacy, a circle that has no beginning and no end.

Hahn symbolizes *sheer inclusiveness*, pointing to an
indeterminate boundary. It embraces 'one' and 'many' and
'whole' and 'part' simultaneously. The beauty of *hahn* is
that ontological antitheses (whole and part) are united in
paradoxical harmony (oneness). The *radical openness* of
hahn underscores tolerance, acceptance, and latitude. The
hahn mind supports the idea of 'both/and' rather than the
notion of 'either/or'. (2004, p. 24)

Park helps us understand that there is no rejection in *hahn*, instead an unconditional acceptance of otherness prevails in it. It points to the communal consciousness of selfhood which permits the paradoxical reality of 'one in many and many in one'. Such thinking is badly needed in our multicultural world, and it is my contention that the formation of communities of faith that are characterized by such ways of thinking is at the heart of pastoral theology in this current era.

In addition to *hahn*, Park juxtaposes *Jung* – a compassionate passion. In explaining this Eastern feeling, Park makes reference to Korean indigenous healers who are 'possessed – called – by a spirit' to sing, dance and perform healing rituals. These shamans experience forms of 'divine sickness', and are able to heal others through their own wounds. Compassion is evoked within these healers as a result of their own experience of illness. There are immediate parallels here with African traditional priest-healers whose calling and activities are described in similar terms. As we have seen (du Bois, 1903) these, in terms of position and function, were the ancestors of the African American preacher. *Jung* is also a feeling of intimacy, amiability and endearment. 'In *jung*', says Park, 'we heal the wounded, the rejected, the discouraged, the discriminated-against, using our own wounds of being discriminated-against and rejected as a medium of healing' (2004, p. 25).

The third essential element of Park's theology of mutual enhancement is the Korean ethic of *mut*. Park describes *mut* as 'the beauty of difference', 'beauty of natural harmony', 'beauty of asymmetry' or 'grace of gentleness' (2004, p. 26). *Mut* emphasizes the importance of difference, of daring to be different. *Mut* inspires work for great reversals.

The people of *mut* bring great reversals through the beauty of grace. How do we, however, enable the last to be the first? It is by changing the vertical line of hierarchy to a horizontal circle of care. In such a circle, the last will be easily the first. We don't destroy the first, but lead them to the circle of love by changing the systems of hierarchy, exploitation and patriarchy. (2004, p. 27)

By drawing on Korean cultural concepts, Park helps us find vision, passion and ideas towards multicultural living.

Pastoral theologians, in my view, are on a journey of creatively imagining a different kind of world community. The scope of this discipline is that wide. To care deeply, truly and theologically in this world today requires expansive vision, deep passion and thoughtful action. We need to envision a healthy world community if our activities are going to be inspired by a broad enough structure. We need a genuine renewal of our minds if we are to be agents of transformation. We need to draw on indigenous 'knowledges' embedded within communities across the globe. We need respectful engagement across our myriad differences to even begin to approximate the manifold wisdom of God in the care of the world.

Questions for further exploration

1 Examine your own cultural context for issues that need to be approached with an intercultural vision of pastoral theology. What are the issues? How does the vision presented address them?

2 How important are Levinas's thoughts for relations between the West and the rest of the world?

3 How does Homer Ashby's work advance intercultural pastoral theology?

4 How important is an economic analysis in the development of pastoral theology?

5 How helpful is Andrew Sung Park's theology in your own context?

Notes

1 See Emmanuel Lartey, *In Living Color: An Intercultural Approach to Pastoral Care and Counselling*, London: Jessica Kingsley, 2003, pp. 33–7.

2 For a useful and succinct historical study that traces the development of pastoral theology in Britain and the United States, see Elaine Graham, *Transforming Practice: Pastoral Theology in an Age of Uncertainty*, London: Mowbray, 1996, pp. 56–82.

3 For an expansive discussion of models, functions and breadth of pastoral care, see Lartey, *In Living Color*.

4 See George Furniss, *Sociology for Pastoral Care*, London: SPCK, 1995.

5 See Graham, *Transforming Practice*; Paul Ballard (ed.), *The Foundations of Pastoral Studies and Practical Theology*, Cardiff: Faculty of Theology, University College, 1986; and James Newton Poling, *Render unto God: Economic Vulnerability, Family Violence and Pastoral Theology*, St Louis, MO: Chalice Press, 2002.

6 The following section draws on material from a chapter I contributed to the supplement to the *Dictionary of Pastoral Care and Counseling* (Hunter (ed.), 1990). See Emmanuel Lartey, 'Globalization, Internationalization and Indigenization in Pastoral Care and Counselling', in Nancy Ramsey (ed.), *Pastoral Care and Counseling: Redefining the Paradigms*, Nashville: Abingdon Press, 2004.

7 See, for example, Michael Wilson, *A Coat of Many Colours: Pastoral Studies of the Christian Way of Life*, London: Epworth Press, 1988.

8 This point has been made to me several times by students from these contexts. See also Huibeng He, 'Teaching Pastoral Care in a Chinese Christian Context', unpublished D.Min. dissertation, Columbia Theological Seminary, 2004; Steve Sangkwon Shim, 'Cultural Landscapes of Pastoral Counseling in Asia: The Case of Korea with a Supervisory Perspective', in James Farris, *International Perspectives on Pastoral Counseling*, New York: Haworth Press, 2002, pp. 77–98

9 David Augsburger coined the term *interpathy* to refer to 'an intentional cognitive envisioning and affective experiencing of another's thoughts and feelings, even though the thoughts rise from another process of knowing, the values grow from another frame of moral reasoning, and the feelings spring from another basis of assumptions' (*Pastoral Counseling across Cultures*, Philadelphia: The Westminster Press, 1986, p. 29). This 'other' comes from another culture, has a different world view and operates often with a different epistemology.

10 See David Tracy, 'The Foundations of Practical Theology' in Don Browning (ed.), *Practical Theology: The Emerging Field in Theology, Church and World*, San Francisco: Harper & Row, 1983, p. 6182.

11 Lartey, *In Living Color*, pp. 131–8.

Bibliography

Chinua Achebe, *Things Fall Apart*, London: Heinemann Educational Books, 1965.

Carroll A. Watkins Ali, *Survival and Liberation: Pastoral Theology in African American Context*, St Louis, Missouri: Chalice, 1999.

Rubem Alves, 'Personal Wholeness and Political Creativity: The Theology of Liberation and Pastoral Care' *Pastoral Psychology*, 1977, Vol. 26 (2), 124–36.

Rex Ambler, 'Where on Earth is God?' in Young (ed.), 1995, pp. 90–9.

Samuel Amirtham (ed.), *A Vision for Man: Essays on Faith, Theology and Society*, Madras: Christian Literature Society, 1978.

Cheryl B. Anderson, *Women, Ideology and Violence: Critical Theory and the Construction of Gender in the Book of the Covenant and the Deuteronomic Law*, London/New York: T & T Clark Int., 2004.

Dale P. Andrews, *Practical Theology for Black Churches: Bridging Black Theology and African American Folk Religion*, Louisville, Kentucky: Westminster John Knox Press, 2002.

Homer U. Ashby, Jr, *Our Home is Over Jordan: A Black Pastoral Theology*, St Louis, Missouri: Chalice Press, 2003.

David W. Augsburger, *Pastoral Counseling across Cultures*, Philadelphia: The Westminster Press, 1986.

Paul H. Ballard (ed.), *The Foundations of Pastoral Studies and Practical Theology*, Cardiff: Faculty of Theology, University College, 1986.

Paul Ballard, 'The Emergence of Pastoral and Practical Theology in Britain' in Woodward and Pattison (eds), 2000.

Paul Ballard & Pam Couture (eds), *Globalisation and Difference: Practical Theology in a World Context*, Cardiff: Cardiff Academic Press, 1999.

Paul Ballard & Pam Couture (eds), *Creativity, Imagination and Criticism: The Expressive Dimension in Practical Theology*, Cardiff: Cardiff Academic Press, 2001.

Paul Ballard & John Pritchard, *Practical Theology in Action: Christian Thinking in the Service of Church and Society*, London: SPCK, 1996.

Sara Baltodano, 'Pastoral Care in Latin America' in Farris (ed.), 2002, 191–224.

Werner Becher, Alastair V. Campbell & G. Keith Parker (eds), *The Risks of Freedom*, Manila, Philippines: The Pastoral Care Foundation Inc. 1993.

Insoo Kim Berg & Ajakai Jaya, 'Different and Same: Family Therapy with Asian-American Families', *Journal of Marital and Family Therapy*, 1993, Vol. 19 (1), 31–8.

Abraham Adu Berinyuu, *Pastoral Care to the Sick in Africa: An Approach to Transcultural Pastoral Theology*, Frankfurt and New York: Peter Lang, 1988.

Abraham Adu Berinyuu, *Towards Theory and Practice of Pastoral Counselling in Africa*, Frankfurt-am-Main, Bern, New York: Peter Lang, 1989.

Stephen B. Bevans, *Models of Contextual Theology*, rev. and expanded edn, Maryknoll, NY: Orbis, 2002.

Homi Bhabha, *The Location of Culture*, London and New York: Routledge, 1994.

Bhagavad-Gita: The Song of God, trans. Swami Prabhavananda and Christopher Isherwood. New York: Harper & Brothers, 1944/1951.

Leonardo Boff and Clodovis Boff, *Introducing Liberation Theology*, Tunbridge Wells: Burns & Oates, 1987.

Elias Bongmba, *African Witchcraft and Otherness*, New York: State University of New York Press, 2001.

Elias Bongmba, 'Eschatology: Levinasian Hints in a Preface' in Tamara Eskenazi *et al.*, 2003, 75–90.

Pierre Bourdien, *The Logic of Practice*, trans. Richard Nice, Stanford, CA: Stamford University Press, 1990.

Don S. Browning (ed.), *Practical Theology: The Emerging Field in Theology, Church and World*, San Francisco: Harper & Row, 1983.

Don S. Browning, *A Fundamental Practical Theology: Descriptive and Strategic Proposals*, Minneapolis: Fortress Press, 1996.

Alastair V. Campbell, *Rediscovering Pastoral Care*, London: Darton, Longman & Todd, 1981.

Alastair V. Campbell, *A Dictionary of Pastoral Care*, London: SPCK, 1987.

Donald Capps, *Biblical Approaches to Pastoral Counseling*, Philadelphia: Westminster Press, 1981.

W. A. Clebsch & C. R. Jaekle, *Pastoral Care in Historical Perspective*, New York: Harper, 1964/1967.

Howard Clinebell, *Basic Types of Pastoral Counseling*, Nashville: Abingdon Press, 1966.

John B. Cobb, Jr & David Ray Griffin, *Process Theology: An Introductory Exposition*, Philadelphia, PA: The Westminster Press, 1976.

Pamela D. Couture & Rodney J. Hunter (eds), *Pastoral Care and Social Conflict*, Nashville: Abingdon Press, 1995.

Philip L. Culbertson & Arthur B. Shippee (eds) *The Pastor: Readings from the Patristic Period*, Minneapolis: Fortress Press, 1990.

Gavin D'Costa, 'Trinitarian *Différance* and World Religions: Postmodernity and the "Other"' in King (ed.), 1998, 28–46.

Colin Davis, *Levinas: An Introduction*, Notre Dame, Indiana: University of Notre Dame Press, 1996.

Jacques Derrida, in Raoul Mortley (ed.), *French Philosophers in Conversation*, London: Routledge, 1991.

Musa W. Dube, *Postcolonial Feminist Interpretation of the Bible*, St Louis, Missouri: Chalice Press, 2000.

W. E. B. du Bois, *The Souls of Black Folk*, New York: Penguin Books, (1903) 1989.

Narciso Dumalagan, Werner Becher & Tazio Taniguchi (eds), *Pastoral Care and Counseling in Asia: Its Needs and Concerns*, Manila: Clinical Pastoral Care Association of the Philippines, 1983.

V. Enriquez, *Indigenous Psychology and National Consciousness: The Philippine Experience*, Tokyo, Japan: Institute for the Study of Languages and Cultures of Asia and Africa, 1994.

Tamara Eskenazi, Gary Phillips & David Jobling (eds), *Levinas and Biblical Studies*, Atlanta: Society of Biblical Literature, 2003a.

Tamara Eskenazi, 'Introduction – Facing the Text as Other: Some Implications of Levinas's Work for Biblical Studies' in Eskenazi *et al.* (eds), 2003b, 1–16.

Tamara Eskenazi, 'Love your Neighbour as An Other: Reflections on Levinas's Ethics and the Hebrew Bible', in Eskenazi *et al.* (eds), 2003, 145–57.

Edward Farley, 'Theology and Practice Outside the Clerical Paradigm' in Browning (ed.), 1982.

Edward Farley, 'Interpreting Situations: An Essay in Practical Theology' in Lewis Mudge & James Poling (eds), *Formation and Reflection: The Promise of Practical Theology*, Philadelphia, PA: Fortress Press, 1987, 1–26.

Edward Farley, *Practicing Gospel: Unconventional Thoughts on the Church's Ministry*, Louisville, KY and London: Westminster John Knox Press, 2003.

James R. Farris, *International Perspectives on Pastoral Counseling*, New York, London and Oxford: The Haworth Press, 2002.

Paul S. Fiddes, *Participating in God: A Pastoral Doctrine of the Trinity*, Louisville, KY: Westminster John Knox Press, 2000.

John Foskett, 'Playing With One Another: Some Reflections on a Visit Down Under', *Contact*, Vol. 96 (2), 1988.

George Furniss, *Sociology for Pastoral Care: An Introduction for Students and Pastors*, London: SPCK, 1995.

Charles V. Gerkin, *The Living Human Document: Re-visioning Pastoral Counseling in a Hermeneutical Mode*, Nashville: Abingdon Press, 1984.

Charles V. Gerkin, *Widening the Horizons: Pastoral Responses to a Fragmented Society*, Philadelphia: The Westminster Press, 1986.

Charles V. Gerkin, *Prophetic Pastoral Practice: A Christian Vision of Life Together*, Nashville: Abingdon Press, 1991.

Charles V. Gerkin, *An Introduction to Pastoral Care*, Nashville: Abingdon Press, 1997.

Robert Gibbs, *Correlations in Rosenzweig and Levinas*, Princeton, NJ: Princeton University Press, 1992.

Fred C. Gingrich, 'Pastoral Counseling in the Philippines: A Perspective from the West' in Farris (ed.), 2002, 5–55.

Nancy Gorsuch, 'Gender as Construct and Category in Pastoral Theology: A Review of Recent Literature', *Journal of Pastoral Theology*, Vol. 10, 2000, 96–111.

Elaine L. Graham, *Transforming Practice: Pastoral Theology in an Age of Uncertainty*, London: Mowbray, 1996.

Larry Kent Graham, *Discovering Images of God: Narratives of Care among Lesbians and Gays*, Louisville, KY: Westminster John Knox Press, 1997.

Laurie Green, *Let's Do Theology: A Pastoral Cycle Resource Book*, London: Mowbray, 1990.

James L. Griffith and Melissa Elliot Griffith, *Encountering the Sacred in Psychotherapy: How to Talk to People about their Spiritual Lives*, New York and London: The Guildford Press, 2002.

Thomas Groome, *Christian Religious Education*, San Francisco: Harper & Row, 1981.

Paul Halmos, *Faith of the Counsellors*, London: Constable, 1965.

James H. Harris, *Preaching Liberation*, Minneapolis: Fortress Press, 1995.

Seward Hiltner, *Preface to Pastoral Theology*, Nashville: Abingdon Press, 1958.

E. Brooks Holifield, *A History of Pastoral Care in America: From Salvation to Self-realization*, Nashville: Abingdon Press, 1983.

Barbara A. Holmes, *Race and the Cosmos: An Invitation to View the World Differently*, Harrisburg, PA: Trinity Press International, 2002.

Rodney Hunter (gen. ed.), *Dictionary of Pastoral Care and Counseling*, Nashville: Abingdon Press, 1990.

Gordon E. Jackson, *A Theology for Ministry: Creating Something of Beauty*, St Louis, Missouri: Chalice Press, 1998.

Charles Jencks (ed.), *The Post-modern Reader*, London: Academy Editions; New York: St Martin's Press, 1992.

BIBLIOGRAPHY

Ted Jennings, 'Pastoral Theological Methodology' in Hunter (gen. ed.), 1990.

Gareth Jones, 'What is Truth? Rehabilitating Pontius Pilate' in Young (ed.), 1995.

Merle R. Jordan, *Taking on the Gods: The Task of the Pastoral Counselor*, Nashville: Abingdon Press, 1986.

Gordon Kaufman, 'Theological Method and Indigenization: Six Theses' in Amirtham (ed.), 1978, 49–60.

Ursula King (ed.), *Faith and Praxis in a Postmodern Age*, London: Cassell, 1998.

Colin Lago & Joyce Thompson, *Race, Culture and Counselling*, Buckingham: Open University Press, 1996.

Robert A. Lambourne, 'Religion, Medicine and Politics', *Contact*, Vol. 44, 1974, 1–40.

Thomas A. Langford, *Practical Divinity: Theology in the Wesleyan Tradition*, Vol. 1, rev. edn, Nashville: Abingdon Press, 1998a.

Thomas A. Langford, *Methodist Theology*, Peterborough: Epworth, 1998b.

Emmanuel Lartey, Daisy Nwachuku & Kasonga wa Kasonga (eds), *The Church and Healing: Echoes from Africa*, Frankfurt, Bern and New York: Peter Lang, 1994.

Emmanuel Y. Lartey, *In Living Color: An Intercultural Approach to Pastoral Care and Counselling*, rev. 2nd edn, London: Jessica Kingsley, 2003.

Simon Yiu Chuen Lee, 'Pastoral Counseling in Chinese Cultural Contexts: Philosophical, Historical, Sociological, Spiritual and Psychological Considerations' in Farris (ed.), 2002, 119–49.

Emmanuel Levinas, *En découvrant l'existence avec Husserl et Heidegger* (Discovering Existence with Husserl and Heidegger), trans. Richard A. Cohen, Bloomington: Indiana University Press, 1949, 1967, 1974.

Emmanuel Levinas, *Totality and Infinity: An Essay on Exteriority*, trans. Alphonso Lingis, Pittsburgh: Duquesne University Press, 1969.

Emmanuel Levinas, *Otherwise than Being or Beyond Essence*, trans. Alphonso Lingis, The Hague: Martinus Nijhoff, 1974 (1981).

Emmanuel Levinas, *Time and the Other*, trans. Richard A. Cohen, Pittsburgh: Duquesne University Press, 1987.

Emmanuel Levinas, *The Levinas Reader*, trans. and ed. Sean Hand, Oxford: Blackwell, 1989.

Lawrence W. Levine, *Black Culture and Black Consciousness*, Oxford, London and New York: Oxford University Press, 1977.

Edgar V. McKnight, 'Varieties of Readings and Interpretations of the Biblical Text', *The New Interpreter's Study Bible: New Revised Standard Version with the Apocrypha*, Nashville: Abingdon Press, 2003, 2268–73.

John McNeill, *A History of the Cure of Souls*, New York: Harper & Row, 1977.

Randy L. Maddox, *Responsible Grace: John Wesley's Practical Theology*, Nashville: Kingswood Books: 1994.

Ram Adhar Mall, *Intercultural Philosophy*, Lanham, MD: Rowman & Littlefield, 2000.

Robert J. S. Manning, *Interpreting Otherwise than Heidegger: Emmanuel Levinas's Ethics as first Philosophy*, Pittsburgh, PA: Dusquesne University Press, 1993.

Jean Masamba ma Mpolo & Wilhelmina Kalu (eds), *Risks of Growth: Counselling and Pastoral Theology in the African Context*, Nairobi: Uzima Press, 1985.

Jean Masamba ma Mpolo & Daisy Nwachuku (eds), *Pastoral Care and Counselling in Africa Today*. Frankfurt, Bern, New York, Paris: Peter Lang, 1991.

Robert B. Mellert, *What is Process Theology?*, New York: Paulist Press, 1975.

L. N. Mercado (ed.) *Filipino Religious Psychology*, Tacloban City, Philippines: Divine Word Publications, 1977.

Bonnie J. Miller-McLemore and Brita L. Gill-Austern (eds), *Feminist and Womanist Pastoral Theology*, Nashville: Abingdon Press, 1999.

Itumeleng J. Mosala, *Biblical Hermeneutics and Black Theology in South Africa*, Grand Rapids, MI: W. B. Eerdmans, 1989.

Wayne E. Oates, *The Presence of God in Pastoral Counseling*, Waco, TX: Word Books, 1986.

Thomas C. Oden, *Pastoral Theology: Essentials of Ministry*, San Francisco: Harper & Row, 1983.

William B. Oglesby, *Biblical Themes for Pastoral Care*, Nashville: Abingdon Press, 1980.

Judith Lynn Orr, 'A dialectical understanding of the psychological and moral development of working-class women with implications for pastoral counseling', unpublished dissertation, Ann Arbor, UMI, 1991.

Andrew Sung Park, *The Wounded Heart of God: The Asian Concept of Han and the Christian Doctrine of Sin*, Nashville: Abingdon Press, 1993.

Andrew Sung Park, *From Hurt to Healing: A Theology of the Wounded*, Nashville: Abingdon Press, 2004.

Andrew Sung Park, 'A Theology of Enhancement: Multiculturality in Self and Community', *Journal of Pastoral Theology*, Vol. 13 (2), 2003, 14–33.

Andrew Sung Park, 'The Formation of Multicultural Religious Identity within persons in Korean-American Experience', *Journal of Pastoral Theology*, Vol. 13 (2), 2003, 34–50.

Pastoral Ministry in a Fractured World: Proceedings of the 3rd International Congress on Pastoral Care and Counseling, Melbourne, Australia: International Council on Pastoral Care and Counseling, 1987.

Stephen Pattison, 'The Use of the Behavioural Sciences in Pastoral Studies' in Ballard (ed.), 1986, 79–85.

Stephen Pattison, *A Critique of Pastoral Care*, 2nd edn, London: SCM Press, 1993.

Stephen Pattison, 'Some Straw for the Bricks: A Basic Introduction to Theological Reflection' in Woodward & Pattison (eds), 2000, 135–45.

John Patton, *Pastoral Care in Context*, Minneapolis: Fortress Press, 1993.

James Newton Poling, *The Abuse of Power: A Theological Problem*, Nashville: Abingdon Press, 1991.

James Newton Poling, *Render unto God: Economic Vulnerability, Family Violence and Pastoral Theology*, St Louis, Missouri: Chalice Press, 2002.

James N. Poling & Donald E. Miller, *Foundations for a Practical Theology of Ministry*, Nashville: Abingdon Press, 1985.

Lynne Price, *Faithful Uncertainty: Leslie D. Weatherhead's Methodology of Creative Evangelism*, Frankfurt-am-main, Berlin, Bern, New York: Peter Lang, 1996.

Karl Rahner & Heinz Schuster, 'Preface', *Concilium* Vol. 3 (1), March 1965, 3.

Rainbow Spirit Elders, *Rainbow Spirit Theology: Towards an Australian Aboriginal Theology*, Melbourne: HarperCollins Religious, 1997.

Nancy Ramsey (ed.), *Pastoral Care and Counseling: Redefining the Paradigms*, Nashville: Abingdon Press, 2004.

Russell E. Richey, with Dennis M. Campbell & William B. Lawrence, *Marks of Methodism: Theology in Ecclesial Practice*, Nashville: Abingdon Press, 2005.

Edward Said, *Orientalism*, London: Penguin Books, 1978, 1985.

R. M. Salazar-Clemena (ed.), *Counseling in Asia: Integrating Cultural Perspectives*, Cebu City, Philippines: Association of Psychological and Educational Counselors of Asia, 2000.

Karen D. Scheib, 'Contributions of Communion Ecclesiology to the Communal Contextual Model of Care', *Journal of Pastoral Care*, Vol. 12 (2), 2002, 28–50.

Chris R. Schlauch, *Faithful Companioning: How Pastoral Counseling Heals*, Minneapolis: Fortress Press, 1995.

Heinz Schuster, 'Pastoral Theology: Nature and Function', *Concilium*, Vol. 3 (1), March 1965, 4–9.

Fernando F. Segovia, *Decolonizing Biblical Studies: A View from the Margins*, New York: Orbis, 2000.

Society for Intercultural Pastoral Care and Counselling, *Human Images and Life-stories in a Multicultural World: Papers of the 9th International Seminar on Intercultural Pastoral Care and Counselling*, Mülheim/Rühr, October 1995.

Robert Solomon, 'The Future Landscape of Pastoral Care and Counseling in the Asia Pacific Region' in Farris (2002), 99–118.

Joseph E. Stiglitz, *Globalization and its Discontents*, New York and London: W. W. Norton & Co., 2002.

R. S. Sugirtharajah (ed.), *Voices from the Margin: Interpreting the Bible in the Third World*, London: SPCK, 1991; New York: Orbis, 1995

R. S. Sugirtharajah (ed.), *The Postcolonial Bible*, Sheffield: Sheffield Academic Press, 1998.

R. S. Sugirtharajah , *Asian Biblical Hermeneutics and Postcolonialism: Contesting the Interpretations*, Sheffield: Sheffield Academic Press, 1999.

R. S. Sugirtharajah , *The Bible and the Third World: Precolonial, Colonial and Postcolonial encounters*, Cambridge: Cambridge University Press, 2001.

R. S. Sugirtharajah , *Postcolonial Criticism and Biblical Interpretation*, Oxford: Oxford University Press, 2002.

R. S. Sugirtharajah , *Postcolonial Reconfigurations: An Alternative Way of Reading the Bible and Doing Theology*, St Louis, Missouri: Chalice Press, 2003.

John V. Taylor, *The Go-Between God: The Holy Spirit and the Christian Mission*, London: SCM Press, 1972.

Paul Tillich, *Systematic Theology*. Vol. 1, London: SCM Press, 1951/1988.

David Tracy, *Blessed Rage for Order: The New Pluralism in Theology*, New York: Seabury, 1975.

David Tracy, 'Practical Theology in the Situation of Global Pluralism' in Lewis Mudge & James Poling, *Formation and Reflection*, Philadelphia: Fortress Press, 1987, 139–54.

Miroslav Volf & Dorothy C. Bass (eds), *Practicing Theology: Beliefs and Practices in Christian Life*, Grand Rapids, MI and Cambridge, UK: Eerdmans, 2002.

Renita Weems, *Battered love: Marriage, Sex and Violence in the Hebrew Prophets*, Minneapolis: Fortress Press, 1995.

Cornel West, *Race Matters*, New York: Vintage Books, 1994.

James D. Whitehead & Evelyn Eaton Whitehead, *Method in Ministry: Theological Reflection and Christian Ministry*, rev. edn, Kansas City: Sheed & Ward, 1995.

James A. Whyte, 'Practical Theology' in Campbell (ed.), 1987, 212–13.

Robert J. Wicks & Barry K Estadt (eds), *Pastoral Counseling in a Global Church*, Maryknoll, NY: Orbis. 1993.

Michael Wilson, *A Coat of Many Colours: Pastoral Studies of the Christian Way of life*, London: Epworth Press, 1988.

Michael Wilson, *Dear Bryony: An Exploration of a Christian Way of Life in the Modern World*, London: Chester House Publications, 1995.

Edward P. Wimberly, *Pastoral Care in the Black Church*, Nashville: Abingdon Press, 1979.

Edward P. Wimberly, *Pastoral Counseling and Spiritual Values: A Black Point of View*, Nashville: Abingdon Press, 1982.

Edward P. Wimberly, *African American Pastoral Care*, Nashville: Abingdon Press, 1992.

Edward P. Wimberly, *Using Scripture in Pastoral Counseling*, Nashville: Abingdon Press, 1994.

Edward P. Wimberly, *Counseling African American Marriages and Families*, Louisville, KY: Westminster John Knox, 1997.

Edward P. Wimberly, *Recalling our Own Stories: Spiritual Renewal for Religious Caregivers*, San Francisco, California: Jossey-Bass, 1997.

Edward P. Wimberly, *Moving from Shame to Self-worth: Preaching and Pastoral Care*, Nashville: Abingdon Press, 1999.

Edward P. Wimberly, *Relational Refugees: Alienation and Reincorporation in African American Churches and Communities*, Nashville: Abingdon Press, 2000.

Edward P. Wimberly, *Claiming God, Reclaiming Dignity: African American Pastoral Care*, Nashville: Abingdon Press, 2003.

Edward P. Wimberly & Anne Streaty Wimberly, *Liberation and Human Wholeness: The conversion experiences of Black People in Slavery and Freedom*, Nashville: Abingdon, 1986.

James Woodward & Stephen Pattison (eds), *The Blackwell Reader in Pastoral and Practical Theology*, Oxford, UK and Malden, MA: Blackwell, 2000.

Gale Yee, 'Ideological Criticism: Judges 17—21 and the Dismembered Body', in Gale Yee (ed.), *Judges and Method: New Approaches in Biblical Studies*, Minneapolis: Fortress Press, 1995, 146–70.

Frances Young, *The Art of Performance: Towards a Theology of Holy Scripture*, London: Darton, Longman & Todd, 1990.

Frances Young (ed.), *Dare We Speak of God in Public?*, London: Mowbray, 1995.